Days to Remember

Devotions for the Holidays Throughout the Year

Henry M. Morris

First printing, November 2005
Second printing, July 2006

ISBN-13: 978-0-89051-472-6
ISBN-10: 0-89051-472-0
Library of Congress Number: 2005936821

Cover by Brent Spurlock

Please visit our website for other great titles:
www.masterbooks.net

For information regarding author interviews,
please contact the publicity department at (870) 438-5288.

Printed in the United States of America

Master
Books
A Division of New Leaf Publishing Group

Acknowledgments

A number of the capable and dedicated secretarial-editorial members of ICR's publications staff have been of real help in the preparation and compilation of devotional Bible studies. These would include Mary Thomas, Kelly Griffin, Leigh Pierce, Ruth Richards, and my daughter, Mary Smith. The final publication, including illustrations, is largely the work of the Master Books staff. I do appreciate greatly all their fine help.

CONTENTS

PREFACE

These brief devotional Bible studies are largely taken from articles in the ICR booklet *Days of Praise*, a periodical which has been issued quarterly beginning in 1986. This devotional booklet is sent free each quarter to those who have requested it, about a quarter million each issue. Judging from their testimonies, God has graciously used it to instruct and encourage many people in the great truths of God's Word.

The sub-title of this third collection, *Devotions for the Holidays throughout the Year*, is self-explanatory. I have been privileged to write special devotionals for each of our main American holidays each year for 20 years, so the total number has become substantial. Not all have been printed here, but each holiday is believed to be well represented.

It may be that some reader will be called on to teach a class on Easter, say, or give a Thanksgiving devotional, or speak on some other holiday, and will find one or another of the devotional studies helpful. I hope so, and also that most readers will want to read them just for their own encouragement on the respective holidays. I know I personally have been blessed in studying the great truths of the relevant Scriptures while preparing them. Most of all, I pray that they are honoring to our gracious Lord and His wonderful words of life.

Chapter I

CHRISTMAS

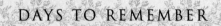

The Christmas season — especially Christmas Day — is observed essentially all over the world as honoring the birthday of Jesus Christ. However, the actual date of Christ's birth — even the year — is still uncertain. Many nations and Christian groups have designated December 25 as the official date, but even this was not done until the 5th century A.D. To some considerable degree, this date was taken over from that of the winter solstice, since no actual record exists as to the true date.

Many Christians — most notably the Puritans of 17th century England — have refused to observe Christmas at all, considering it (with considerable evidence) as having originated in pagan festivals associated with the winter solstice. The fact is, of course, that no one yet knows for sure when Jesus' birth in Bethlehem really took place, and the existing festivals in late December seemed like a convenient choice.

In any case, His birth was *not* when He actually left heaven. His incarnation, beginning with His miraculous conception in the womb of the Virgin Mary, was when the eternal Word of God first became flesh. In fact, the term "Christmas," often defined in modern times as the "mass" of Christ, really means "Christ-sent" (the word "mass" itself was derived from the same Latin word from which we get such words as "mission" and "missionary"). Thus, the Son of God was *sent* on a great mission into the world that He had created thereby to become also the Son of Man, thereafter living in sinless perfection as God intended man to live. He could then redeem lost men and women by the sacrifice of himself. It is then the *incarnation*, rather than the birth itself, which is the vital message at the season we call Christmas.

THE PROMISED SEED OF THE WOMAN — A VERY SPECIAL SON

"The book of the generation of Jesus Christ, the son of David, the son of Abraham" (Matt. 1:1).

These opening words of the New Testament identify this "book of the generation (literally "*genesis*") of Jesus Christ" as telling of the wonderful fulfillment of the promise to both Abraham and David of a very special Son. To Abraham, God had promised: "Because thou hast done this thing, and hast not withheld thy son, thine only son . . . in thy seed shall all the nations of the earth be blessed; because thou hast obeyed my voice" (Gen. 22:16–18). This prophecy was directed immediately through Abraham's son Isaac, but focused finally on Jesus Christ, Abraham's greater Son. "Now to Abraham and his seed were the promises made. He saith not, And to seeds, as of many; but as of one, And to thy seed, which is Christ" (Gal. 3:16).

Similarly, a unique promise was made to David concerning his own special Son. "I will set up thy seed after thee. . . . I will be His Father, and He shall be My Son. . . . And thine house and thy kingdom shall be established for ever before thee" (2 Sam. 7:12–16). Once again, this promise applied precursively to Solomon, but ultimately to the greater Son of David, "made of the seed of David according to the flesh, And declared to be the Son of God with power . . . by the resurrection of the dead" (Rom. 1:3–4). He was greater than Abraham, greater than David, and even "better than the angels. . . . For unto which of the angels said He at any time . . . I will be to Him a Father, and He shall be to me a Son?" (Heb. 1:4–5). Further, He was the fulfillment of the primeval promise of the coming "seed of the woman" (Gen. 3:15). He is the virgin's Son (Isa. 7:14), the Son given (Isa. 9:6), "the last Adam. . . . the Lord from heaven" (1 Cor. 15:45–47).

"The book of the generations of Adam" (Gen. 5:1) introduces the Old Testament, with its record of human failure and God's promises. "The book of the generation of Jesus Christ" introduces the New Testament and the fulfillment of the promises, culminating in eternal redemption through the Son of David, the Son of Abraham, the Son of God!

A NEW THING CREATED

"How long wilt thou go about, O thou backsliding daughter? for the LORD hath created a new thing in the earth, A woman shall compass a man" (Jer. 31:22).

Long ago, the "Preacher" in great wisdom concluded: "There is no new thing under the sun" (Eccles. 1:9). This is also the opinion of the leaders of the modern intellectual establishment who will be saying in the last days: "All things continue as they were from the beginning of the creation" (2 Pet. 3:4).

But God reminds us, as He reminded His backsliding people of Israel, that He has, indeed, created one new thing in the earth. Since only God can "create" (wherever this verb occurs in the Bible, God is the subject), a really *new* thing (not just a new combination of existing things) would have to be produced directly by the Lord himself. Of course, God had completed His original work of creating all things long ago (Gen. 2:1–3), including a marvelous mechanism for human reproduction. Nevertheless, because of man's sin, He very soon had to begin a work of reconciliation, and this included a primeval promise that the seed of the woman (Gen. 3:15) would come someday to accomplish this great work. Since all normal reproduction requires the male seed, such a miracle would mean God would have to create a new thing when the appropriate time would come. At that time, as Isaiah prophesied many years later, "*the* virgin shall conceive, and bear a son," and that Son would be "the mighty God," who would establish His kingdom "with justice from henceforth even for ever" (Isa. 7:14; 9:6–7).

Then, still later, Jeremiah reminded his forgetful people of this same great promise. God would *create*, by His mighty power, a *new thing*, a perfect human body, without inherited sin or physical blemish, and with no contribution from either male or female, in the womb of a specially called virgin. She would compass that "holy thing" (Luke 1:35) with warmth and love for nine long months as it grew in her womb. Then, in the fullness of time, "God sent forth His Son, made of a woman" (Gal. 4:4) to "save His people from their sins" (Matt. 1:21).

THE ETERNAL SON OF GOD

But thou, Bethlehem Ephratah, though thou be little among the thousands of Judah, yet out of thee shall He come forth unto me that is to be ruler in Israel; whose goings forth have been from of old, from everlasting" (Mic. 5:2).

This is a very remarkable prophecy, explicitly predicting, some 700 years before He finally came, that the future king of Israel would be born in the little village of Bethlehem. Humanly speaking, Micah would probably have guessed the place of His birth would be Jerusalem, the great capital of Judah. Then, to assure its fulfillment, the Roman Emperor Augustus had to decree a comprehensive census, compelling Joseph to take Mary with him to Bethlehem for her child to be born.

That the prophecy involves an actual child birth is clear not only from the phrase "come forth," but also from the succeeding verse, which warns that God will "give them up, until the time that she which travaileth hath brought forth" (Mic. 5:3). The preceding verses had also predicted that "they shall smite (this coming ruler) the judge of Israel with a rod upon the cheek" (Mic. 5:1), speaking of His initial rejection and execution.

That is not all. The prophecy not only foresees His birth in Bethlehem, His repudiation by His own people, and His eventual installation as king over all Israel (not merely Judah), but also that this same remarkable person was none other than God himself. His "goings forth" had been "from everlasting." That is, He is eternally proceeding forth from His Father. He did not become God's Son when He was born in Bethlehem; He has been coming forth eternally. "The only begotten Son, which is in the bosom of the Father, He hath declared Him" (John 1:18).

There is still another truth implied in the remarkable Hebrew word for "goings-forth." It is also used for such things as the flowing of water from a fountain or the radiations from the sun. Thus, the never-ending flowing forth of power from God through the Son is nothing less than the sustaining energy for the whole creation, as He is "upholding all things by the word of His power" (Heb. 1:3). This was to be the babe in Bethlehem!

A CHILD BORN
AND A SON GIVEN

"For unto us a child is born, unto us a son is given: and the government shall be upon His shoulder: and His name shall be called Wonderful, Counsellor, The mighty God, The everlasting Father, The Prince of Peace" (Isa. 9:6).

This magnificent verse, used so often on Christmas cards, is a splendid prophecy of the divine/human nature of the coming Messiah. He would be *born* as a child, like every other human being, but He would also be *given* as a Son at the same time, with the giver clearly being God himself. "He *gave* His only begotten Son!" (John 3:16).

The name of this God/man offers further testimony. At the introduction of this prophecy, God had named Him *Immanuel*, meaning "God with us" (Isa. 7:14). Now He is given a series of names, all of which are needed to express His full identity. It is likely the first two names should be considered one name: He is our "Wonderful Counselor" (the punctuation marks have been added to our translations, but the combined term is more in keeping with the structure of the other names).

This "child," amazingly, is also "The mighty God" and "The everlasting Father," stressing His absolute and eternal deity, as well as His omnipotence and the unity of the Father and the Son in the triune godhead. Finally, as "The Prince of Peace," it is only He that can unite the warring factions of mankind and bring true world peace. These names stress His deity, but also His perfect and effective humanity.

Also, in His human nature, He is our "Wonderful Counselor," our perfect example and infallible teacher. He both shows and tells us what to believe and how to live, and He is never wrong, for in Him "are hid all the treasures of wisdom and knowledge," and "in him dwelleth all the fulness of the Godhead bodily" (Col. 2:3, 9).

THE SCEPTRE
OF JUDAH

"The sceptre shall not depart from Judah, nor a lawgiver from between his feet, until Shiloh come; and unto him shall the gathering of the people be" (Gen. 49:10).

This is a remarkable Messianic prophecy, given by Jacob 1,700 years before the first coming of Christ fulfilled it. Later prophecies would focus on His descent from David and then His birthplace in Bethlehem, but first one of the 12 sons of Jacob must be designated as His progenitor.

Remarkably, Jacob did not select either his firstborn son, Reuben, or his favorite son, Joseph. Nor did he choose Benjamin, the son of his favorite wife. He chose instead his fourth son, Judah, evidently by divine direction.

Yet it was over 600 years before the tribe of Judah gained ascendancy over the others. The greatest leaders of Israel were from other tribes — Moses and Samuel from Levi, Joshua from Ephraim, Gideon from Manasseh, Samson from Dan, and Saul from Benjamin. Finally, David became king, and "the sceptre" was then held by Judah for a thousand years until Jesus was born in Bethlehem of Judea. Jesus' parents were both of Judah, both of the line of David, with both the legal and spiritual right to David's throne. Then, just 70 years after His birth, "the sceptre" (that is, leadership over the 12 tribes) departed from Judah with the worldwide dispersion of Israel, and no man since has ever held that right. It is still retained by Jesus, and will be reclaimed and exercised when He returns.

In the meantime, the prophecy stands as an unchallengeable identification of Jesus as the promised Messiah. Ancient Jewish commentators all recognized "Shiloh" as a name for Messiah. Since the sceptre has already departed, Shiloh has already come. When He returns, His people will, indeed, finally be gathered together "unto Him."

Joseph —
The Fruitful Bough

"Joseph is a fruitful bough, even a fruitful bough by a well; whose branches run over the wall" (Gen. 49:22).

This is part of Jacob's dying prophetic blessing on his 12 sons. Each of the 12 prophecies has been fulfilled, including this prediction of Joseph's fruitfulness.

Joseph actually received a double inheritance in the future land of Israel, with the two tribes of Ephraim and Manasseh both descended from him. The name Joseph means "increasing," so that even his name was prophetic of the great multitudes who would be his descendants.

There is another interesting and intriguing fulfillment of this prophecy. More men were named after Joseph than any other man in the Bible, with no less than 11 different "Josephs" mentioned in Scripture. This may not seem so remarkable until it is realized that no one else in the Bible was named after Adam or Noah, Abraham or Isaac, or even Moses or David or Solomon. No one was named after Paul or Peter. Why, then, so many Josephs (except to fulfill prophecy)? One would normally think that Abraham or Moses or David would provide the most favored names for Hebrew children, but not so.

Among all the namesakes of Joseph, the most important were Joseph (the husband of Mary) and Joseph of Arimathea. One provided legitimacy to the birth of Jesus, taking the virgin Mary as his wife and giving Jesus the legal right to David's throne. The other provided a legitimate burial to Jesus, falsely condemned and crucified as a criminal.

Two Josephs — both descended from Judah rather than from their namesake — thus played key roles at the beginning and end of the earthly ministry of the true "increaser," the "Child born" and the "Son given." He is the most fruitful branch of all, for "Of the increase of His government and peace there shall be no end" (Isa. 9:6–7).

PARABLE OF
THE STAR

"I shall see him, but not now: I shall behold him, but not nigh: there shall come a Star out of Jacob, and a Sceptre shall rise out of Israel, and shall smite the corners of Moab, and destroy all the children of Sheth" (Num. 24:17).

A parable is not an illustrative story, as most people think, but a "dark saying" (note Ps. 78:2), designed to reveal some hidden truth only to those who are prepared to understand (note Jesus' assertion in Matt. 13:10–17).

The first reference in the Bible to parables is in connection with the seven parables of the false prophet Balaam (Num. 23:7, 18; 24:3, 15, 20, 21, 23). The central parable of these seven verses is the one in our text speaking of a mysterious Star which would come out of Jacob and a Sceptre out of Israel, both the Star and the Sceptre representing a great person coming in the far future, destined both to guide and to rule all nations.

The wise men of the East somehow recognized His star when it began rising, and came seeking the King. The star they saw, appearing perhaps in one of the constellations long associated by ancient peoples with the primeval promise of a coming redeemer/king — was but a type of the true "bright and morning star" (Rev. 22:16) and the "day star" that one day shall "arise in your hearts" (2 Pet. 1:19), that "light of the world" (John 8:12) who would be "the light of life" for all people who follow Him in faith.

He would also be the Sceptre, the King of all kings, that "rod of iron" by which all nations must one day be ruled (Rev. 19:15) in righteousness. The babe in Bethlehem would become the suffering servant on the Cross, then would rise from the grave like a bright and morning star out of the darkness and now will also very soon be acknowledged as "the blessed and only Potentate, the King of kings, and Lord of lords" (1 Tim. 6:15).

BALAAM, A VERY FAMOUS prophet from Mesopotamia, was possibly a true prophet of God at one time, but through greed became a false prophet when the king of Moab hired him to curse Israel, the chosen people of God. God constrained him instead to prophesy a Star that would come someday to announce the coming of a Savior and King who would arise in Israel and eventually rule the whole world (see Num. 22–24).

THE OPENED EAR
AND THE FATHER'S WILL

"Sacrifice and offering thou didst not desire; mine ears hast thou opened: burnt offering and sin offering hast thou not required" (Ps. 40:6).

That Psalm 40 is primarily a Messianic psalm speaking mainly about the work of Christ is evident from its quotation as such in Hebrews 10:5–10. The psalm is prophesying particularly of His incarnation, as He says: "Lo, I come: in the volume of the book it is written of me" (Ps. 40:7).

Burnt offerings and sin offerings were indeed required from God's people under the law, but these were not an end in themselves. These sacrifices were meaningless unless they were offered out of a willing heart, obedient expressions of submission to a forgiving God.

That was the implication of the "opened ear," a symbolic expression indicating one's willingness thenceforth to hear only the voice of his master and to submit to His will in all things. If a freed bondservant "shall plainly say, I love my master . . . I will not go out free: Then his master shall . . . bore his ear through with an aul; and he shall serve him for ever" (Exod. 21:5–6). This was the testimony of the coming Messiah, as reported in our text.

Then note its application as recorded in Hebrews 10:5: "Wherefore when he cometh into the world, he saith, Sacrifice and offering thou wouldest not, but a body hast thou prepared me." That is, the phrase, "mine ears hath thou opened," would be translated by the Holy Spirit as "a body hast thou prepared me." The perfect submission of the Son to the Father required that He become a man, with a very special human body prepared by His Father. Then Psalm 40:7 becomes (in Heb. 10:7): "Lo, I come . . . to do thy will, O God." "By the which will we are sanctified through the offering of the body of Jesus Christ once for all" (Heb. 10:9–10).

Lo, I Come

"Then said I, Lo, I come (in the volume of the book it is written of me,) to do thy will, O God" (Hebrews 10:7).

The marvelous words of Hebrews 10:5–7 are an interpretive quotation from Psalm 40:6–8, which in turn was cited prophetically as the testimony of the eternal Son of God as He prepared to leave heaven and "the bosom of the Father" (note John 1:18) to descend to earth to become also "the Son of man," with no "where to lay His head" (Matt. 8:20).

He would first take up residence on earth in the womb of Mary, then in a manger, then a house in Bethlehem, then somewhere in Egypt until the death of King Herod who would seek to kill Him, then in the home of His foster father in a despised village, eventually on a cross on which His enemies would impale Him, and finally for three days in a borrowed tomb.

All this, amazingly, would be simply to do the will of His Father in heaven, which He fully understood would include the terrible death of the Cross. "Therefore doth my Father love me, because I lay down my life, that I might take it again" (John 10:17).

We can never comprehend such love — only believe it and receive it. "For God so loved the world, that he gave his only begotten Son, that whosoever believeth in him should not perish, but have everlasting life" (John 3:16). Now we can testify with Paul: "the life which I now live in the flesh I live by the faith of the Son of God [*His* faith, not ours!], who loved me, and gave himself for me" (Gal. 2:20).

Anyone who ignores that love should note this sobering truth: "He that believeth not is condemned already, because he hath not believed in the name of the only begotten Son of God" (John 3:18).

GARMENTS FOR
THE KING

"All thy garments smell of myrrh, and aloes, and cassia, out of the ivory palaces, whereby they have made thee glad" (Ps. 45:8).

One of the most beautiful of the Christmas hymns (though rarely sung at Christmas) is "Out of the Ivory Palaces," telling how the King of heaven left His heavenly home and laid aside His perfumed, royal clothing to enter "a world of woe." That this 45th Psalm is symbolic in part is obvious; but that it refers to Christ is also obvious from its use in Hebrews 1:8: "But unto the Son He saith, Thy throne, O God, is for ever and ever: a sceptre of righteousness is the sceptre of thy kingdom," quoting Psalm 45:6.

That the eternal King left heaven to come to earth is not symbolic, however, but very real; nor did He have royal robes in which to be arrayed, for they "wrapped [Him] in swaddling clothes" and laid Him "in a manger" (Luke 2:12).

Then, as He later walked the dusty roads of Judea, we know little of what He wore, but we do know that on one notable occasion, He "laid aside his garments; and took a towel, and girded himself. . . . and began to wash the disciples' feet" (John 13:4–5). A strange garment, and stranger action, for the King of glory!

Yet stranger still that men whom He had created, later "took his garments, and made four parts, to every soldier a part; and also his coat. . . . but cast lots for it" (John 19:23–24), leaving Him naked to die a painful death spiked to a tree. Finally, His little remnant of friends took "the body of Jesus, and wound it in linen clothes" (John 19:40) for His burial.

Now, however, in glory, He once again is arrayed in kingly apparel, "clothed with a garment down to the foot, and . . . with a golden girdle" (Rev. 1:13), and one day, all His redeemed shall see Him — in His beauty — the King in whose law we delight!

The Word
Made Flesh

"And the Word was made flesh, and dwelt among us, (and we beheld his glory, the glory as of the only begotten of the Father,) full of grace and truth" (John 1:14).

This is the definitive verse on the divine incarnation, when "God was in Christ, reconciling the world unto himself" (2 Cor. 5:19), and the wealth of truth implied therein is beyond human comprehension. We can never understand how the infinite God could become finite man, but where the intellect fails, faith prevails.

It was the Word who "was God" and by whom "all things were made" (John 1:1, 3), yet He made His own human body, in the womb of Mary, and therein "dwelt among us" for 33 years. The Greek word here for "dwelt" is unusual, literally meaning "tabernacled."

How could this be? "Without controversy great is the mystery of godliness: God was manifest in the flesh, justified in the Spirit, seen of angels, preached unto the Gentiles, believed on in the world, received up into glory" (1 Tim. 3:16). This is, indeed, a great mystery, "but with God all things are possible" (Matt. 19:26). God made a body for Adam; surely He could also make a perfect body in which He himself could "tabernacle." He was made "in the likeness of sinful flesh" (Rom. 8:3) and "was in all points tempted [i.e., 'tested'] like as we are, yet without sin" (Heb. 4:15). Since "God cannot be tempted with evil" (James 1:13), and since the Word, who was God, was merely tabernacling in the likeness of sinful flesh, this testing was to demonstrate to man (not to himself) that He was without sin and therefore able to save sinners. Therefore, John could testify: "We *beheld* his glory!"

Jesus Christ is, indeed, true man — in fact, He is man as God intended man to be. Neither in the womb of Mary, nor on the Cross, did He ever cease to be God.

THE LIKENESS OF
SINFUL FLESH

"For what the law could not do, in that it was weak through the flesh, God sending his own Son in the likeness of sinful flesh, and for sin, condemned sin in the flesh" (Rom. 8:3).

The great truth of Christmas (meaning, originally, "Christ-sent") is that "God was manifest in the flesh" (1 Tim. 3:16). The eternal Word, "was made flesh, and dwelt among us" (John 1:14). So vital is this truth that "every spirit that confesseth not that Jesus Christ is come in the flesh is not of God; and this is that spirit of antichrist . . . and even now already is it in the world" (1 John 4:3).

Jesus Christ is the God/man — infinite God and perfect man, perfectly joined in full union, and salvation is based on this truth. If Jesus Christ were not perfect man, He could not die for the sins of man; if He were not God, He could not defeat death and save us from the penalty of sin.

He could not be born in *sinful* flesh, of course, like all the descendants of Adam, but only in the "likeness" of sinful flesh. From the moment of conception, He must be "holy, harmless, undefiled, separate from sinners" (Heb. 7:26), and thus miraculously conceived in a virgin's womb.

In fact, that miraculous creation of His body in the womb of Mary was the actual moment when God became man. It is even possible that the incarnation took place on about the very night that we now call Christmas; since it is probable that Jesus was actually *born* in the early fall, when shepherds were in the field with their sheep. It may even have been on Michaelmas ("Michael sent"), the fall holiday on September 29, honoring the angel who with the heavenly host announced the birth of Jesus on that night long ago. How appropriate it would be if "the light of the world" had indeed come into the world on or near that world's longest night just nine months before.

THE TRUE HUMANITY
OF JESUS

"Hereby know ye the Spirit of God: Every spirit that confesseth that Jesus Christ is come in the flesh is of God" (1 John 4:2).

The great truth associated with Christmas is the glorious fact of the incarnation, that the eternal Word of God, without whom "was not any thing made that was made" (John 1:3) "was made flesh, and dwelt among us" (John 1:14). The Bible warns, therefore, that anyone who denies the human nature of Christ "is not of God" but rather is of the "spirit of antichrist" (1 John 4:3).

This problem is very real because "many false prophets are gone out into the world" (1 John 4:1) — that is, those "New Age" teachers, gurus, rabbis, and mullahs who deny that Jesus and the Christ are eternally one, and that the Lord Jesus Christ died for our sins and rose again, and that this was a physical death and bodily resurrection.

The real message of Christmas is not about a baby or gift-giving or good will, though these elements are all there, but about the God/man, who once came "in the likeness of sinful flesh" to die in our place, and thereby "condemned sin in the flesh" (Rom. 8:3). It will not do to say that any person can become a "Christ" or any other compromise that dilutes either the humanity or the deity of the Lord Jesus Christ. As the apostle John testified, "For the life was manifested, and we have seen it, and bear witness, and shew unto you that eternal life, which was with the Father, and was manifested unto us" (1 John 1:2).

That living Word of God "was made in the likeness of men . . . and became obedient unto death, even the death of the cross. Wherefore God also hath highly exalted him. . . . That at the name of Jesus every knee should bow . . . And that every tongue should confess that Jesus Christ is Lord, to the glory of God the Father" (Phil. 2:7–11).

THE
GOD-MAN

"Concerning his Son Jesus Christ our Lord, which was made of the seed of David according to the flesh; and declared to be the Son of God with power, according to the Spirit of holiness, by the resurrection from the dead" (Rom. 1:3–4).

How Christ could be both man and God is a great mystery, but the fact that He *is* both man and God is certain, both from Scripture and from history. This "hypostatic [substantive] union" is set forth in many passages of Scripture, including this one. He was "made" to be a man, by placing the body of flesh "prepared" for Him by God (Heb. 10:5) in the womb of the virgin, who was herself descended from David. Then He was "declared" to be the Son of God by His mighty resurrection from the dead, an event beyond the power of any but God himself to accomplish.

A similar testimony is found in Galatians 4:4: "But when the fulness of the time was come, God sent forth his Son, made of a woman, made under the law." As deity, He was "sent forth" from God in heaven. In His humanity, He was "made of a woman." His "being in the form of God" preceded His taking upon himself "the form of a servant" (Phil. 2:6–7). As the eternal Word, He "was God," but He "was made flesh, and dwelt among us" (John 1:1, 14).

The same truth is found even in the Old Testament Messianic prophecies. "For unto us a child is born, unto us a Son is given" (Isa. 9:6). As a child, He must be *born,* but as God's Son, He would be *given.* Furthermore, that human child would also be the "mighty God" and the "everlasting Father." "A virgin shall conceive, and bear a son, and shall call his name Immanuel" ("God with us"; Isa. 7:14).

Christ *has* eternally been God; He *will* eternally be man. He *is,* forever, the God-man — man as God intended man to be and also the one true, eternal God.

JESUS WAS AND IS a true man — in fact, a sinless man but otherwise a man like other men, but He was always, from eternity, the Son of God, in perfect union with God the Father. Eventually however, He became the Son of Man. Henceforth He will always be the God-man. Note especially John 1:1–3, 14, and Philippians 2:5–11.

WHAT IT COST FOR GOD TO BECOME MAN

"Thou madest him a little lower than the angels; thou crownedst him with glory and honor, and didst set him over the works of thy hands" (Heb. 2:7).

We cannot comprehend what it meant for the infinite Creator God to become finite man, even coming "in the likeness of sinful flesh" (Rom. 8:3). Nevertheless, we can, and must, believe it, for "every spirit that confesseth not that Jesus Christ is come in the flesh is not of God" (1 John 4:3).

The Scriptures have given us a glimpse of the "emptying" that His incarnation required, the setting aside of certain outward aspects of His deity. He had been "so much better than the angels" (Heb. 1:4), but He had to be "made a little lower than the angels for the suffering of death" (Heb. 2:9). Angels do not die, but He who was "the Life" (John 14:6) must be "put to death in the flesh" (1 Pet. 3:18).

He was the eternal Word who "was God" (John 1:1), but it was necessary that "the Word was made flesh" (John 1:14). "The world was made by him" (John 1:10), but "the princes of this world . . . crucified the Lord of glory" (1 Cor. 2:8).

He, "being in the form of God, thought it not robbery to be equal with God" (Phil. 2:6). That is, He was not fearful of losing His deity and, therefore, did not have to cling to His divine nature and attributes as He became man. Thus, He "made himself of no reputation" (emptying himself of the outward form of God), "and took upon him the form of a servant" (Phil. 2:7). From the glorious form of God to the humble form of a human slave — this is the measure of what it meant for God to become man.

Yet that was only the beginning. "For he hath made him to be sin for us, who knew no sin; that we might be made the righteousness of God in him" (2 Cor. 5:21). He suffered hell for us, that we might enjoy heaven with Him.

Because He was willing to be so humiliated, He will one day be crowned with glory and honor. "God also hath highly exalted him . . . that every tongue should confess that Jesus Christ is Lord" (Phil. 2:9–11).

WHY JESUS CAME DOWN FROM HEAVEN

"And no man hath ascended up to heaven, but he that came down from heaven, even the Son of man which is in heaven" (John 3:13).

At the Christmas season, even the secular world makes much of the Christ child, born in a manger, but few ever seem to recognize that He had been eternally one with the Father in heaven before He chose to come down. Even fewer stop to learn just *why* He chose to come down. As a matter of fact, He had much to say on this subject, giving many reasons why He came. Note just a few of them.

The first reference in the New Testament on this great theme, coming from His own lips, is very significant. "Think not that I am come to destroy the law, or the prophets: I am not come to destroy, but to fulfill" (Matt. 5:17). His total commitment to God's written Word was the first thing He came to confirm!

There are so many other reasons He has given for His coming that we can just list a small part of them, but note these especially.

"For the Son of man is come to seek and to save that which was lost" (Luke 19:10).

"I came not to call the righteous, but sinners to repentance" (Luke 5:32).

"Think not that I am come to send peace on earth: I came not to send peace, but a sword" (Matt. 10:34).

"For I came down from heaven, not to do mine own will, but the will of him that sent me" (John 6:38).

"I am come that they might have life, and that they might have it more abundantly" (John 10:10).

The last time Christ gives a reason for His coming is also very significant. It refers to His *second* coming! "Behold, I come quickly; and my reward is with me, to give every man according as his work shall be" (Rev. 22:12).

THE
SECOND MAN

"The first man is of the earth, earthy: The second man is the Lord from heaven" (1 Cor. 15:47).

Paleoanthropologists, seeking to trace man's supposed evolutionary ancestry, have widely different opinions as to the when and how of it. As one evolutionist has recently lamented: "Paleoanthropologists seem to make up for a lack of fossils with an excess of fury, and this must now be the only science in which it is still possible to become famous just by having an opinion."

There is no need to speculate. The Bible solves the problem when it speaks of "the first man Adam" (1 Cor. 15:45) and says that Eve "was the mother of all living" (Gen. 3:20). There were no "pre-Adamite men" (as even some Christians have alleged, hoping thereby to accommodate evolutionary speculations).

Adam, alone, was "the first man," and he had been formed directly by God "of the dust of the ground" (Gen. 2:7) — that is, out of the same basic elements as those in the earth (carbon, oxygen, hydrogen, etc.). He was "earthy," like the materials of earth. But, then, how could Jesus Christ, who is "the Lord from heaven," be "the second man?" Adam had millions of male descendants before Jesus was born.

The answer can only be that He was "the second man" in the same way that Adam was "the first man." That is, His human body, like that of Adam, was directly made by God, from earth's elements — not produced by reproduction, like all other men. He was "made flesh" (John 1:14), but only made "in the *likeness* of *sinful* flesh," for He must not inherit the sinful flesh of His human parents, if He is to "condemn sin in the flesh" (Rom. 8:3). "A body hast thou prepared me," He said (Heb. 10:5), and as the angel told Mary: "That holy thing which shall be born of thee shall be called the Son of God" (Luke 1:35).

THE SAVIOR
OF THE WORLD

"And we have seen and do testify that the Father sent the Son to be the Saviour of the world" (1 John 4:14).

This unique title of the Lord Jesus Christ assures us that, when the Father sent His Son away from the glories of heaven down to a world lost in sin, it was not just to be the Messiah of the Jews, or to assume David's throne as king of Israel, or to punish the wicked Gentile nations.

"For God sent not his Son into the world to condemn the world; but that the world through him might be saved" (John 3:17).

In fact, this special title is used only one other time in the Bible, and it was used by Samaritans rather than Jews when they came to know Jesus as He ministered among them for two days. These people were mostly of Gentile background with a mixture of Israeli blood who had become adherents of a quasi-Jewish religion that was also part pagan.

They were actually looking for a Savior, and their testimony after meeting Jesus was: "Now we believe . . . and know that this is indeed the Christ, the Saviour of the world" (John 4:42). They perceived that He had come to bring salvation to lost sinners in every nation, not just to Israel or Samaria. As He said later "I came not to judge the world, but to save the world" (John 12:47).

So He commanded His disciples "that repentance and remission of sins should be preached in his name among all nations" (Luke 24:47). He became to the Father "the propitiation . . . for the sins of the whole world" (1 John 2:2), when He offered up His life as a sacrifice for sins, then died and rose again. We who have believed on Him as our personal Savior are now to be His witnesses "in all Judaea, and in Samaria, and unto the uttermost part of the earth" (Acts 1:8).

Signs of Christmas

"Moreover the LORD spoke again unto Ahaz, saying, Ask thee a sign of the LORD thy God; ask it either in the depth, or in the height above" (Isa. 7:10–11).

Although "the Jews require a sign" (1 Cor. 1:22), and this attitude was rebuked by Christ when He said that "an evil and adulterous generation seeketh after a sign" (Matt. 12:39), God has given three specific signs with respect to the incarnation of Christ. There were other signs too, no doubt, such as the star of Bethlehem, but three events were specifically called signs.

First, to the unwilling King Ahaz, He said: "Therefore the LORD himself shall give you a sign; Behold, a virgin shall conceive, and bear a son, and shall call his name Immanuel" (Isa. 7:14). Immanuel means "God with us," and the sign of the virgin birth, biologically impossible without a mighty miracle of divine creation, assures us that the omnipotent God has entered the human family once for all.

That entrance was not made in an emperor's palace as a great conqueror, however, but in the very humblest of human circumstances, and this also was a sign. "And this shall be a sign unto you," said the leader of the angelic host; "Ye shall find the babe wrapped in swaddling clothes, lying in a manger" (Luke 2:12).

There was a third sign. When the infant Jesus was brought to the temple, the aged prophet Simeon said, "Behold, this child is set for the fall and rising again of many in Israel; and for a sign which shall be spoken against . . . that the thoughts of many hearts may be revealed" (Luke 2:34–35).

That is, the God/man would himself be God's great sign to Israel and the whole world. The attitude of men and women to God, in Christ, would reveal the state of their hearts and seal their eternal destiny, whether rising again to everlasting life or falling forever away from God.

THE VIRGIN
BIRTH

"Therefore the LORD himself shall give you a sign: Behold, a virgin shall conceive, and bear a Son, and shall call his name Immanuel" (Isa. 7:14).

This has been a hotly disputed verse, as unbelievers for two thousand years have tried to undermine the vital doctrine of the unique sinlessness of Christ. Without the miraculous conception and virgin birth of Jesus, not only is His mother Mary made to be an impure woman, but also Jesus is deprived of His intrinsic deity, being born with the sin-nature inherited from Adam. He could not really be our sin-bearing Savior since He would thus be sinful also.

Because of this intrinsic importance of the virgin birth to the very essence of Christianity, liberals and other opponents of the truth have long argued that the Hebrew *almah* should be translated "young woman," instead of "virgin." This is utterly wrong, of course. There would be no "sign" in a "young woman conceiving," and it would be blasphemous to name an ordinary child Immanuel ("God with us"), clearly implying divine incarnation in man.

Even if *almah* could legitimately be thus translated, none of its seven occurrences in the Old Testament *require* any meaning other than "virgin." The issue is settled for all who believe the Bible by the fact that the Holy Spirit inspired Matthew to use *parthenos* (a Greek word which can *only* mean "virgin") when he translated and quoted Isaiah 7:14 (see Matt. 1:23, "Behold, a *virgin* shall be with child"). Actually, both Isaiah 7:14 and Matthew 1:23 support the use of the definite article ("Behold, *the* virgin . . .") in this great prophecy. God has, indeed, "sent forth his Son, made of a woman" (Gal. 4:4), and *only* of a woman, fulfilling the primeval promise of "the seed of the woman" who would someday bring deliverance from Satan and sin and death (Gen. 3:15).

Mary and
the Grace of God

"And the angel said unto her, Fear not, Mary: for thou hast found favor with God" (Luke 1:30).

This announcement by the angel Gabriel to the virgin Mary, that she had been chosen as the mother of the coming Savior, contains the first mention in the New Testament of the Greek word for "grace" *(charis)*. Mary was chosen, not for anything she had done, but because she had "found grace."

In a remarkable parallel, certainly implying divine inspiration, the first mention of "grace" in the Old Testament is also associated with the coming of a new dispensation in God's dealings with men. "But Noah found grace in the eyes of the LORD" (Gen. 6:8).

Just as Mary found grace, so Noah had found grace. Grace is not something one earns or purchases; grace is a treasure that is *found!* When a person — whether Noah or Mary or someone today — finally realizes that salvation is only by the grace of God, received through faith in the saving work of Christ, he or she has made the greatest discovery that could ever be made, for it brings eternal life.

There is an even greater dimension to the grace of God. When we do "find" grace, it is actually because God in His infinitely precious grace has found us, and revealed to us the Savior of our souls. Just as God found Moses in the desert, and found Paul on the road to Damascus, then saved and called them to His service, so He finds us, and then we also find His saving grace.

Mary's discovery of God's grace in salvation, through the coming of the "seed of the woman" into the world, is revealed in her *Magnificat.* "My soul doth magnify the Lord, and my spirit hath rejoiced in God my Saviour" (Luke 1:46–47). This could well have also been the testimony of Noah long ago, and it surely should be the testimony of each of us who has found grace today.

WHEN THE ANGELS WORSHIPED CHRIST

"And again, when he bringeth in the first begotten into the world, he saith, And let all the angels of God worship him" (Heb. 1:6).

Jesus Christ is "the only begotten Son, which is in the bosom of the Father" (John 1:18), but the day finally came when He had to proceed all the way to earth, and the eternal Word "was made flesh, and dwelt among us, (and we beheld His glory, the glory as of the only begotten of the Father,) full of grace and truth" (John 1:14). A few years later, He would be "declared to be the Son of God . . . by the resurrection from the dead" (Rom. 1:4). By eternal generation, by the incarnation, by the virgin birth, and by the resurrection, He is in every sense God's "first begotten" — His only begotten — Son.

Our text says that when He first entered the world, born of the virgin, His Heavenly Father called on all the innumerable angels in the heavenly host to bow down and worship Him. It is not clear whether this command is a quotation from the Old Testament or not, although it is cited in a passage which also quotes several other Messianic prophecies as applied to Jesus Christ. Psalm 97:7 and Deuteronomy 32:43 have been suggested as possible source verses, but neither of these seems to fit very well in context. Thus, it may be that our text refers directly, and solely, to a specific decree of God, proclaimed throughout the universe at the time of the human birth of His Son, and recorded here alone.

All the angels of the infinite cosmos bowed in solemn worship, but a special contingent was commissioned to watch directly over the birth, and proclaim the good news to those nearby. "And suddenly there was with the angel a multitude of the heavenly host praising God, and saying, Glory to God in the highest, and on earth peace, good will toward men" (Luke 2:13–14).

The angels saw and worshiped; the shepherds heard and told. "And all they that heard it wondered" (Luke 2:18).

SHEPHERDS IN
THE FIELD

"And there were in the same country shepherds abiding in the field, keeping watch over their flock by night" (Luke 2:8).

The date of Christ's birth, as observed in the Western world, is December 25, although other dates have been observed at various times and places — in January, March, May, etc. Actually, no one really knows. In fact, the church did not observe it at all for the first two centuries. The date in late December which was eventually adopted coincided with the various pagan festivals held in connection with the winter solstice.

A significant clue is found in our text. Shepherds were almost certainly not abiding in the fields watching over their flocks in late December; the sheep would have been gathered into the sheep folds long before that.

Another possible clue is the recorded presence of "the angel of the Lord" (verse 9) to announce the birth of the Savior, along with a "multitude of the heavenly host" (verse 13). The angel leading the host was likely Michael the archangel (note Jude 9). The angel Gabriel, who stands "in the presence of God" (Luke 1:19), was sent to bear individual messages to Zacharias and Mary (Luke 1:11, 26, 27), but Michael is the one seen commanding the angelic host (Rev. 12:7).

It may be significant that the ancient church in Britain observed a date called Michaelmas (i.e., "Michael sent"), known as the feast of Michael and the angels. This date (still recognized in England's legal system) is September 29 — a date when it is reasonable that Jewish shepherds would be in the fields with their flocks. Now, if that might be the date of Christ's birth, then December 25 (nine months earlier) could well be the real date of the incarnation, when the eternal Creator God left heaven to take up residence as a special "seed" in a virgin's womb!

IT WAS POSSIBLY MICHAEL, "the great prince which standeth for the children of thy people" (Dan. 12:1) who led the heavenly host as they announced the birth of Christ to the shepherds (Luke 2:8–14). He had left heaven's "ivory palaces" (Ps. 45:8) to live nine months in the virgin's womb, thence to be "lying in a manger" (Luke 2:16) for a brief time, and eventually to die on a cross. But the day will come when "every knee" will bow to Him and "every tongue" will acknowledge that "Jesus Christ is Lord" (Phil. 2:10–11).

JOY TO
THE WORLD

"And the angel said unto them, Fear not: for, behold, I bring you good tidings of great joy, which shall be to all people" (Luke 2:10).

When God became man, and Jesus was born, true joy entered a world of sin and sadness. The Magi, who had been long anticipating the Savior's coming, "rejoiced with exceeding great joy" when they saw the star standing over the young child (Matt. 2:10). This is the first mention of "joy" in the New Testament.

The heavenly host also rejoiced as their angelic captain shared with the shepherds in the field at Bethlehem the "good tidings [that is, 'the gospel'] of great joy." The very gospel we are to preach is a gospel of exceeding joy, because we have a Savior to preach — Christ the Lord!

Although He was "a man of sorrows, and acquainted with grief" (Isa. 53:3), the Lord Jesus "for the joy that was set before Him endured the cross" (Heb. 12:2). He prepared His disciples for His coming death and their own subsequent sufferings for His name's sake by conveying to them His own joy. "These things have I spoken unto you, that my joy might remain in you, and that your joy might be full" (John 15:11). He prayed for them to the Father, "that they might have my joy fulfilled in themselves" (John 17:13). He promised to answer prayers offered to the Father in His name "that your joy may be full" (John 16:24).

Thus, it is that all who truly believe on Christ can testify with Peter that even though "now [we] see Him not, yet believing, [we] rejoice with joy unspeakable and full of glory" (1 Pet. 1:8). Even when suffering for Him, Christians know that "when his glory shall be revealed, [we] may be glad also with exceeding joy" (1 Pet. 4:13), for His Word promises that He will "present [us] faultless before the presence of his glory with exceeding joy" (Jude 24).

TROUBLE AND JOY

"When they saw the star, they rejoiced with exceeding great joy" (Matt. 2:10).

The familiar story of Herod and the wise men, in addition to its important record of some of the events surrounding the birth of Christ, is a fascinating parable of how news of the person and work of the Lord Jesus Christ so effectively separates people into two great companies. The "gospel" of Christ means, literally, "good news," but most people, sad to say, react as though it were bad news.

When the "wise men from the east" came searching for the newborn Savior, this glorious news was received badly right where it should have been received most gladly. "When Herod the king had heard these things, he was troubled, and all Jerusalem with him" (Matt. 2:3). Herod was an Edomite, representing the Romans, but the Jewish leaders were equally unresponsive. The priests and scribes, knowing the prophetic promises, could tell the king where Christ would be born (Matt. 2:5–6), but they were merely "troubled" along with others in Jerusalem. Neither Herod nor the Jewish leaders were glad for the news, and neither would join in looking for the Savior. Later, they all tried to slay Him.

The wise men, on the other hand, "rejoiced with exceeding great joy" (Matt. 2:10) when they found Him. After worshiping Him, "they departed into their own country another way" (Matt. 2:12), no doubt with lives changed as well as itineraries.

One's attitude of heart is all important. Those who proclaim Christ encounter two reactions: "To the one we are the savour of death unto death; and to the other the savour of life unto life" (2 Cor. 2:16). Some, like Herod, react with fear and hatred, setting about to destroy the gospel by persecution. Others in the scholarly community — like the priests and scribes — seem to react with learned indifference but, when confronted more directly with their own hypocrisy, also eventually resort to persecution. But always, there are some who, like the wise men, fall down in joyous faith to worship Him (Matt. 2:11).

THE GIFTS OF
THE WISE MEN

"And when they were come into the house, they saw the young child with Mary his mother, and fell down, and worshipped him: and when they had opened their treasures, they presented unto him gifts; gold, and frankincense, and myrrh" (Matt. 2:11).

These wise men (or Magi) were of great eminence in the Parthian Empire at that time, and it is unlikely that the caravan from the East consisted of only three men. They more likely had a large entourage as they came searching for the future king of Israel, so it was small wonder that "all Jerusalem" was "troubled," along with king Herod (Matt. 2:3). The Parthians (i.e., Persians) had never been conquered by the Romans and at that very time were posing a significant threat along the eastern boundary of the extended Roman Empire.

When they found the young child and His mother in Bethlehem, the Magi "fell down, and worshipped Him" (Matt. 2:11). Why did they offer Him just three gifts — and why *these* three gifts? Somehow, they seemed to have sensed, possibly from meditating deeply on the ancient prophecies of Balaam (Num. 24:17), Daniel (Dan. 9:24–26), and David, concerning the priesthood order of Melchizedek (Ps. 110:4), that this young child whose birth had been announced by a star was destined not only to be the King but would also become the Messianic sacrifice to "make reconciliation for iniquity" (see Dan. 9:24, 26) and then eventually become our eternal High Priest who "ever liveth to make intercession for them" (Heb. 7:25). Thus, the gold would acknowledge His right to reign; the frankincense would speak of the incense to be offered in the heavenly tabernacle, and the myrrh (John 19:39) to testify that His crucified body would be so anointed as it entered the tomb for a very temporary burial.

THE
MAN CHILD

"And she brought forth a man child, who was to rule all nations with a rod of iron: and her child was caught up unto God, and to his throne" (Rev. 12:5).

This remarkable scene was part of a great vision given to the apostle John as the Lord was revealing to him "the things which shall be hereafter" (Rev. 1:19). He had seen an amazing "sign" in heaven — a woman "clothed with the sun . . . travailing in birth," with "a great red dragon" awaiting the delivery and ready "to devour her child as soon as it was born" (Rev. 12:1–4).

Although the whole vision is richly symbolic, the figure of the man child clearly refers to Jesus Christ, because it is He alone who must eventually rule all nations "with a rod of iron" (Rev. 19:15). Thus, the symbolic "woman" must suggest His human mother Mary but also Eve, the "mother of all living" (Gen. 3:20), for in His human birth, the Son of God became also "the Son of man" (Acts 7:56; Rev. 1:13). The vision, in fact, dramatizes the long warfare between the great dragon (i.e., Satan — Rev. 12:9) and the seed of the woman (Gen. 3:15).

In the vision, the "man child" will have been "caught up" (i.e., "raptured") to heaven, and the dragon and his angels "cast out" to earth (Rev. 12:5, 9). When Christ returns from heaven, all believers, living and dead, will also be "caught up" to meet Him in the air, and thus may well be included in the man child of the great "sign."

There has been continuous warfare between the seed of the serpent and the spiritual seed of the woman ever since the beginning. The dragon is forever "wroth with the woman" and with "the remnant of her seed, which keep the commandments of God, and have the testimony of Jesus Christ" (Rev. 12:17). Christ will finally prevail and cast Satan into the eternal lake of fire (Rev. 20:10).

A LIGHT
TO THE GENTILES

"And he said, It is a light thing that thou shouldst be my servant to raise up the tribes of Jacob, and to restore the preserved of Israel: I will also give thee for a light to the Gentiles, that thou mayest be my salvation unto the end of the earth" (Isa. 49:6).

These words were presumably directed to the Son by the Father as the triune God prepared to implement the ancient promise that a Savior would come to bring salvation to a world lost in sin. That salvation would not only be the restoration of Israel as God's elect nation, but also would reach the Gentile nations and spread to the ends of the earth.

The old prophet Simeon referred to this prophecy when he took up the infant Jesus in his arms, and said, "Lord, now lettest thou thy servant depart in peace. . . . For mine eyes have seen thy salvation, Which thou hast prepared before the face of all people; A light to lighten the Gentiles, and the glory of thy people Israel" (Luke 2:29–32).

Similar prophecies occur in other Old Testament passages as well. "I the Lord have called thee in righteousness, and will hold thine hand, and will keep thee, and give thee for a covenant of the people, for a light of the Gentiles" (Isa. 42:6). "Arise, shine; for thy light is come, and the glory of the Lord is risen upon thee. . . . And the Gentiles shall come to thy light, and kings to the brightness of thy rising" (Isa. 60:1–3). The latter verse apparently prophesies even the coming of the Magi to worship the child Jesus in Bethlehem.

Paul used this truth as he preached to Gentiles in Antioch and elsewhere. "So hath the Lord commanded us, saying, I have set thee to be a light of the Gentiles, that thou shouldst be for salvation unto the ends of the earth" (Acts 13:47; also note Acts 26:23). In fact, Jesus not only enlightens both Jews and Gentiles, but is "the light of the world" (John 8:12).

THE DAYSPRING
FROM ON HIGH

"Through the tender mercy of our God; whereby the dayspring from on high hath visited us" (Luke 1:78).

This is an unusual but beautiful name for the coming Savior given Him by Zacharias when he was "filled with the Holy Ghost, and prophesied" (Luke 1:67). In that same prophecy, Zacharias also called that coming one "the Highest" and "the Lord" who would "give knowledge of salvation unto his people by the remission of their sins" (verses 76–77). Just six months later, Jesus was born.

The Greek word here translated "dayspring" is so translated only this one time. It refers to the metaphorical spring from which the sun springs forth each day, and so is usually translated simply as "the east." It is interesting that it is used three times in connection with the story of the wise men "from the east" who saw "his star in the east" and then, when they reached Bethlehem once again, "the star, which they saw in the east," led them to the one who was himself "the dayspring" (Matt. 2:1, 2, 9).

There is one other sunrise appropriately presaged here. Many years later, the women who had tearfully watched the Lord being crucified and buried came to His sepulcher to anoint Him with sweet spices "at the rising of the sun" (Mark 16:2) immediately after He had risen from the dead. Here a closely related word is the word translated "rising."

There is another great sunrise coming, as promised in the last chapter of the Old Testament. "But unto you that fear my name shall the Sun of righteousness arise with healing in his wings" (Mal. 4:2). He who is himself "the light of the world" (John 8:12) will someday even replace the sun in the new Jerusalem. There will never be another sunrise after that, for "there shall be no night there . . . neither light of the sun; for the Lord God giveth them light" (Rev. 22:5).

THE GREATEST GIFT

"For God so loved the world, that he gave his only begotten Son, that whosoever believeth on him should not perish, but have everlasting life" (John 3:16).

It is singularly appropriate that we look at this greatest of all verses on Christmas Day, for it records the greatest of all gifts. John 3:16 is surely the best known, most loved verse in the Bible, and it has been by far the most effective verse in illuminating blinded minds and breaking hardened hearts, to bring them to Christ and salvation.

The theme of giving is very prominent in the Bible, with such words as "give," "gift," "gave," etc., occurring more than 2,100 times. The first is Genesis 1:17, when God created the sun, moon, and stars "to give light upon the earth," and the last is Revelation 22:12, when Christ will return with His rewards, to "give every man according as his work shall be."

The greatest gift clearly was when God gave himself for a lost and undeserving world. It was the greatest gift because it met the greatest need, revealed the greatest love, and had the greatest scope and greatest purpose of any gift that could ever be conceived in the heart of an omniscient Creator.

That was not the end of His giving, of course. "He that spared not his own Son, but delivered him up for us all, how shall he not with him also freely give us all things?" (Rom. 8:32). "Trust . . . in the living God, who giveth us richly all things to enjoy" (1 Tim. 6:17).

This great gift of God is abundantly sufficient to provide salvation and everlasting life for the whole world. A gift only becomes a gift when it is accepted, and the greatest of all tragedies is that this greatest of all gifts has been spurned and even ridiculed, or — worst of all — simply ignored, by multitudes who need it so greatly. When they brazenly refuse God's free gift of everlasting life, they can only perish in everlasting death. God did all He could do when He gave His Son to suffer and die to save their lost souls.

THE BLESSED HOPE

"Teaching us that, denying ungodliness and worldly lusts, we should live soberly, righteously, and godly, in this present world; Looking for that blessed hope, and the glorious appearing of the great God and our Saviour Jesus Christ" (Titus 2:12–13).

The annual remembrance at Christmastime of the first coming of Christ into the world ought naturally to lead to anticipation of His second coming. To the unbeliever, that coming will entail a fiery time of judgment, but to the Christian, the return of Christ is "that blessed hope." Since the time of the Second Coming is unknown, the Lord has commanded us always to be watchful. "Therefore, be ye also ready," He said (Matt. 24:44).

By no means, however, is this promise conducive to Christian indolence, as some have charged. It encourages us, rather, to "live soberly, righteously, and godly." As John says: "Abide in him; that, when he shall appear, we may have confidence, and not be ashamed before him at his coming" (1 John 2:28). Jesus warned, "Take heed to yourselves, lest at any time your hearts be overcharged with surfeiting, and drunkenness, and cares of this life, and so that day come upon you unawares" (Luke 21:34). How distressing would be the shame of a Christian to be caught in some such situation when his Lord returns!

The hope of His imminent coming is also a great incentive to evangelism and missions. In Paul's last message, immediately after his long description of the last days, he says, "I charge thee therefore before God, and the Lord Jesus Christ, who shall judge the quick and the dead at his appearing and his kingdom; Preach the word . . . do the work of an evangelist" (2 Tim. 4:1–5). Similarly, at the conclusion of his great chapter on the future resurrection at the Second Coming, Paul says: "Therefore . . . be ye steadfast, unmoveable, always abounding in the work of the Lord" (1 Cor. 15:58). Jude, also in the context of the imminent return of Christ, urges us: "And of some have compassion, making a difference: And others save with fear, pulling them out of the fire" (Jude 22–23). The blessed hope is, in fact, a quickening incentive in the Christian life. "And every man that hath this hope in him purifieth himself, even as he is pure" (1 John 3:3).

Chapter II

EASTER

To the Christian, the annual Sunday observance of Easter means commemoration of the bodily resurrection of the Lord Jesus Christ, who rose from the grave on that "first day of the week" after His crucifixion almost 2,000 years ago. The latter is believed to have taken place on the previous Friday (although there have been a number of strong advocates of either Wednesday or Thursday as the day of His death), and so that day has been traditionally called "Good Friday." The previous Sunday, when He first came into Jerusalem for His last week — variously known commonly as Holy Week or Passion Week — is called "Palm Sunday." These three days all have profound spiritual significance, even though there has long been controversy as to calendrical matters.

The year of Christ's death and resurrection is tied, of course, to the date of His birth, which itself is controversial, though probably between 8 and 2 B.C. In general, the Bible indicates that Jesus lived about 33½ years before dying for our sins. He then defeated death and Satan, rising on the third day.

As far as the calendar date of His resurrection is concerned — and thus the date for observing Easter — this also has been extremely controversial over the years ever since, and still is. In Western Christendom, it is now usually designated as the first Sunday following the full moon that occurs on or after March 21st, or the vernal equinox, and so ranges anywhere from March 22 to April 25. Attempts have been made, so far unsuccessfully, to get the nation to agree on a fixed date annually.

Some Christian groups do not observe Easter at all. Like Christmas, its origin has pagan connections associated with the annual spring festivals. The name itself is apparently derived from that of the Teutonic goddess of spring, variously rendered as Eastre or Eastra. Some think it is also connected with the Babylonian goddess Ishtar or the Greek Astarte.

To the first Christians, all of whom were Jews, it was naturally associated with the Jewish Passover, since Jesus had observed the Passover supper with His disciples the night before His arrest and crucifixion. The word "Easter" does appear in Acts 12:4 in the King James and some earlier versions, but it is actually *pasch* in the Greek, which is properly rendered everywhere else as "Passover." Consequently, it usually takes place near the annual time of Passover observance by the Jews.

In any case, the main emphasis is on the resurrection of Christ, which is the real foundation of the Christian faith. In fact, the very reason for observing our weekly "sabbath" (meaning "rest") on Sunday instead of Saturday is to celebrate His resurrection. We thereby commemorate not only the completion of His work of creation (note Exod. 20:8–11) but also the completion of His work of redemption (noted by His victory cry on the cross, "It is finished!" — John 19:30).

These devotional studies are not concerned particularly with dates or such things, but rather with the profound spiritual and doctrinal significance of the death and resurrection of the Lord Jesus Christ.

THE FIRST PALM SUNDAY

"And [Jesus] saith unto them, Go your way into the village over against you: and as soon as ye be entered into it, ye shall find a colt tied, whereon never man sat; loose him, and bring him" (Mark 11:2).

On that first Palm Sunday, over 1,960 years ago, the Lord Jesus fulfilled the ancient prophecy of Zechariah 9:9: "Rejoice greatly, O daughter of Zion; shout, O daughter of Jerusalem: behold, thy King cometh unto thee: He is just, and having salvation; lowly, and riding upon an ass, and upon a colt the foal of an ass." Always before, so far as all records indicate, Jesus walked wherever He went.

Now He must ride! So He borrowed, from some unknown friend in the village, an ass's colt, upon which He could enter the city of the great King.

Although Jesus' circumstances seemed far too lowly for Him to claim a throne, He did indeed come, having salvation for the few who would receive Him. Most of the people, of course, and almost all their leaders, crowned Him only with thorns, and then made a cross His throne.

There was one who recognized Him, however. The colt He requested was a colt "whereon never man sat," and one can be sure that such a colt could not be ridden by any ordinary man without vehement protest and rejection.

Once long ago, the Lord had opened the mouth of an ass and "the dumb ass speaking with man's voice forbad the madness of the prophet" (2 Pet. 2:16). The animals were originally created to be under man's dominion (Gen. 1:26–28), and it was only the entrance of sin into the world that caused the dread of man to come on them (Gen. 9:2). When the true Son of Man and true King of creation calls, then the creatures of the animal kingdom respond, even though His human creatures, whom He loves most of all, still refuse to submit to His rule.

ZECHARIAH'S
STRANGE PROPHECY

"All this was done, that it might be fulfilled which was spoken by the prophet, saying, Tell ye the daughter of Sion, Behold, thy King cometh unto thee, meek, and sitting upon an ass, and a colt the foal of an ass" (Matt. 21:4–5).

When Jesus rode into Jerusalem on an unbroken donkey colt on that momentous first day of the week, just a week before His resurrection, the multitudes quickly recognized that He was fulfilling an ancient prophecy and thereby specifically claiming to be their long awaited Messiah. The prophecy was that of Zechariah 9:9 and, the people in turn began to fulfill David's even more ancient prophecy, laying palm branches in His path, and crying out: "Blessed be he that cometh in the name of the LORD" (Ps. 118:26).

This is one of the few events in the life of Christ that are recorded in all four Gospels, though only Matthew notes it as the fulfillment of prophecy. What a strange prophecy it was! One would think that the anticipated King would come riding on a great white horse, ready to put down all His enemies (and indeed He shall do exactly that some day — see Rev. 19:11).

Here He comes riding on a colt, the foal of an ass, not high and mighty, but meek and lowly! Ah, but as Zechariah prophesied, He comes "just, and having salvation" (Zech. 9:9). The salvation He was bringing was not deliverance from Roman subjugation, but eternal deliverance from sin and its awful wages.

These same multitudes which hailed Him soon were following their high priest in clamoring for His crucifixion. Nevertheless, He someday will fulfill Zechariah's later prophecy: "They shall look upon me whom they have pierced, and they shall mourn for him" (Zech. 12:10). Then, finally, indeed, "The LORD shall be king over all the earth" (Zech. 14:9).

ONE OF THE MOST unusual prophecies (Zech. 9:9) predicted to the Jews that "thy King" would someday come into Jerusalem "having salvation," though not as a conquering warrior, but "lowly," riding not on a great white steed but on "a colt the foal of an ass." More than four centuries later, it was literally fulfilled. We can be confident that His promise to come again "in the clouds of heaven with power and great glory" (Matt. 24:30) will likewise be literally fulfilled.

BRANCHES OF
PALM TREES

"And many spread their garments in the way: and others cut down branches off the trees, and strawed them in the way" (Mark 11:8).

The account of the "triumphant entry" of the Lord Jesus on that first Palm Sunday is one of the few events in the life of Christ that is recorded in all four Gospels. As He rode into Jerusalem on a donkey's colt, deliberately fulfilling the ancient Messianic prophesy of Zechariah 9:9 ("Behold, thy King cometh unto thee . . . just, and having salvation; lowly, and riding upon . . . the foal of an ass"), many of the common people were ready to receive Him as their promised Messiah, trying to lay a kingly carpet for Him as He rode.

Mark's account says they "spread their garments in the way: and . . . branches off the trees," and Matthew's account says essentially the same, adding that "a very great multitude" was doing this (Matt. 21:8). Luke says that "they spread their clothes in the way" (Luke 19:36).

Only John notes that the tree branches which were spread as a carpet were from the palm tree. He records that the people "Took branches of palm trees, and went forth to meet him" (John 12:13). Hence, the name Palm Sunday, the day itself being just one week before His resurrection. All four Gospels note that the multitudes called out as He rode by: "Blessed be the King that cometh in the name of the Lord."

Their leaders all rebuked the people and soon were able to persuade them to call for His blood. "They answered all the people, and said, His blood be on us, and on our children" (Matt. 27:25).

So it has been. The week began with such promise, only to end in rejection and hatred. So Jesus, weeping over Jerusalem, had to say: "O Jerusalem . . . Ye shall not see me henceforth, till ye shall say, Blessed is he that cometh in the name of the Lord" (Matt. 23:37–39).

BELIEVERS AND PALM TREES

"The righteous shall flourish like the palm tree: he shall grow like a cedar in Lebanon" (Ps. 92:12).

Believers are often likened to trees in Scripture. "He shall be like a tree planted by the rivers of water, that bringeth forth his fruit in his season; his leaf also shall not wither; and whatsoever he doeth shall prosper" (Ps. 1:3). "I am like a green olive tree in the house of God" (Ps. 52:8). "His branches shall spread, and his beauty shall be as the olive tree, and his smell as Lebanon" (Hos. 14:6).

The palm tree figure is especially intriguing. In Scripture, the palm is always the date palm, stately and beautiful. It has extremely deep tap roots and thus can flourish even in the desert, growing tall and living long. It is perhaps the most useful of all trees, not only producing its dates, but also sugar, wine, honey, oil, resin, rope, thread, tannin, and dyestuff. Its seeds are fed to cattle and its leaves used for roofs, fences, mats, and baskets. Its fruit is said to get sweeter as the tree grows older, and this is compared to the believer in a beautiful verse: "Those that be planted in the house of the LORD shall flourish in the courts of our God. They shall still bring forth fruit in old age; they shall be fat and flourishing" (Ps. 92:13–14).

It was palm branches that provided a pleasant path for the Lord Jesus as He rode into Jerusalem on the ass's colt on that first Palm Sunday long ago (John 12:13; Matt. 21:8). This, itself, was a picture in miniature of the great multitude of the redeemed and resurrected saints who will greet the Lord Jesus at His throne, "clothed with white robes, and palms in their hands," crying "Salvation to our God which sitteth upon the throne, and unto the Lamb" (Rev. 7:9–10).

May God enable each of us to flourish like the palm tree — beautiful in the Lord, useful in His service, bearing good fruit to His glory, even into old age! At the same time, may God enable us to "be strong in the Lord, and in the power of his might" (Eph. 6:10), like the stately and fragrant cedars of Lebanon.

HOSANNA

"And the multitudes that went before, and that followed, cried, saying, Hosanna to the Son of David: Blessed is he that cometh in the name of the Lord; Hosanna in the highest" (Matt. 21:9).

This was the shout of the throngs as Jesus entered Jerusalem for His last week of public ministry. Even though the multitudes were shouting His adoration, these were the same throngs that would be calling for His crucifixion just a few days later. Nevertheless, as they welcomed Him into Jerusalem that day, spreading palm branches and their own garments in His path, little did they know that they were fulfilling an ancient prophecy.

"Save now, I beseech thee, O LORD. . . . Blessed be he that cometh in the name of the LORD" (Ps. 118:25–26), they cried.

"Save now, I beseech thee, O Lord," is essentially the meaning of "Hosanna." The crowds were acknowledging Jesus as the promised Messiah, the Son of David, and the "chief priests and scribes . . . were sore displeased" at this (Matt. 21:15). This also had been predicted in the psalm: "The stone which the builders refused is become the head stone of the corner. This is the LORD's doing; It is marvellous in our eyes" (Ps. 118:22–23).

It was these "builders" — "the chief priests and elders" — who "persuaded the multitude that they should ask Barabbas, and destroy Jesus" (Matt. 27:20). As a result of this repudiation by these leaders of His people, the Lord wept over Jerusalem, and was forced to prophesy its coming judgment, quoting once again this ancient prophecy: "O Jerusalem, Jerusalem. . . . Behold, your house is left unto you desolate. For I say unto you, Ye shall not see me henceforth, till ye shall say, Blessed is he that cometh in the name of the Lord" (Matt. 23:37–39).

One day He will, indeed, be made the great "head stone of the corner," and all His people will acknowledge Him in that day. In the meantime, the prayer of the prophecy is appropriate for each unsaved person to pray today: "Save *now*, O Lord," thus acknowledging that Jesus has, indeed, come in the Lord's name. "Behold, now is the accepted time; behold, now is the day of salvation" (2 Cor. 6:2).

THE TWO GREATEST WEEKS

"Rejoice greatly, O daughter of Zion; shout, O daughter of Jerusalem: behold, thy King cometh unto thee: He is just, and having salvation; lowly, and riding upon an ass, and upon a colt the foal of an ass" (Zech. 9:9).

The two greatest events in all history are the creation and the redemption of the world. Each of these events involved a great divine week of work and a day of rest. Creation week accomplished the work of the world's formation; the week that is called Holy Week, or Passion Week (perhaps a better term would be Redemption Week), accomplished the work of world salvation.

It is fascinating to compare the events of the seven days of creation week and redemption week, respectively, so we shall do this very briefly in the devotional study for today and, then, day by day.

The first day of creation week involved the very creation of the universe itself (Gen. 1:1). An entire cosmos responded to the creative fiat of the maker of heaven and earth. Initially, this space-mass-time (i.e., heaven, earth, beginning) continuum was created in the form of basic elements only, with no structure and no occupant (Gen. 1:2), a static suspension in a pervasive, watery matrix (2 Pet. 3:5). When God's Spirit began to move, however, the gravitational and electro-magnetic force systems for the cosmos were energized. The waters and their suspensions coalesced into a great spherical planet and, at the center of the electro-magnetic spectrum of forces, visible light appeared (Gen. 1:3).

In a beautiful analogy, on the first day of redemption week, the Creator King of the universe entered His chosen capital city (Matt. 21:1–9) to begin His work of redemption, as He had long ago entered His universe to begin His work of creation. All the basic components of creation were there to acknowledge their Creator. The stones would have cried out for Him (Luke 19:39–40), the branches of the palm trees provided a carpet for Him (John 12:13; Mark 11:8), the ass's colt became His chariot (see our text, Zech. 9:9), and the common people sang His praises (Matt. 21:9). "Behold, thy King cometh unto thee!"

THIS IS
THE DAY

"This is the day which the LORD hath made; we will rejoice and be glad in it" (Ps. 118:24).

This familiar verse is often quoted, or sung, on the Lord's Day, or perhaps some other special day. In context, however, it refers to the day on which the Lord's people would see Him and cry out in joy: "Blessed be he that cometh in the name of the LORD" (Ps. 118:26).

This is exactly what happened on that first "Palm Sunday," when Jesus rode on the colt into Jerusalem, and the multitude began to praise God, saying, "Blessed be the King that cometh in the name of the Lord" (Luke 19:38).

The Jewish leaders, however, and the city as a whole repudiated this response, and it soon became evident that they would seek to destroy Him. He wept over the city, "Saying, If thou hadst known, even thou, at least in this thy day, the things which belong unto thy peace! but now they are hid from thine eyes. . . . because thou knewest not the time of thy visitation" (Luke 19:42–44).

"At least in this thy day. . . . the time of thy visitation." This was the day the Lord had made — the day prophesied for centuries — the day when Messiah would enter the Holy City as its King. They would not have Him, and the Lord Jesus sadly had to pronounce coming judgment on them. "O Jerusalem, Jerusalem, thou that killest the prophets . . . how often would I have gathered thy children together . . . and ye would not! Behold, your house is left unto you desolate. . . . Ye shall not see me henceforth, till ye shall say, Blessed is he that cometh in the name of the Lord" (Matt. 23:37–39).

This will happen when Christ returns. In the meantime, this can be a wonderful experience for each individual who will say from his heart: "Blessed is He who comes *to me* in the name of the LORD," receiving Him by faith. *That* day, for him, indeed will be "the day that the LORD hath made."

Preparation of the Father's House

"And he taught, saying unto them, Is it not written, My house shall be called of all nations the house of prayer? but ye have made it a den of thieves" (Mark 11:17).

As we compare the corresponding days of creation week and redemption week, we must note that the chronology of the latter has been the subject of much disagreement among authorities. Although some details are uncertain, we can at least consider this possible additional dimension to the understanding and harmony of the two weeks.

Having created and activated the earth on the first day, God next provided for it a marvelous atmosphere and hydrosphere in which, later, would live the birds and fishes. No other planet is equipped with air and water in such abundance; the earth was uniquely planned for life! The hydrosphere, on the second day, was further divided into waters below and waters above "the firmament" (Hebrew *raqia,* "stretched-out space"). The waters above the firmament probably consisted of a vast blanket of transparent water vapor, maintaining a perfect climate worldwide, with ideal conditions for longevity.

Paralleling the primeval provision of life-sustaining air and water, on day two of redemption week, the Lord entered again into the city (having spent the night in Bethany) and into the temple, which He had called His Father's house (John 2:16). As He approached the city, He cursed the barren fig tree (Mark 11:12–14) and then, in the temple, overthrew the tables of the moneychangers (Mark 11:15–19). Both actions — the cursing of the fig tree and the cleansing of the temple — symbolize the purging of that which is barren or corrupt in the Creator's kingdom. He had created a world prepared for life (air for the breath of life and water as the matrix of life), but mankind, even the very teachers of His chosen people, had made it unfruitful and impure. As physical life must first have a world of pure air and water, so the preparations for a world of true spiritual life require the purifying breath of the Spirit and the cleansing water of the Word, preparing for the true fruit of the Spirit and the true temple of God's presence, in the age to come.

THE SEA
AND THE MOUNTAINS

"For verily I say unto you, That whosoever shall say unto this mountain,
Be thou removed, and be thou cast into the sea; and shall not doubt in
his heart, but shall believe that those things which he saith shall come
to pass; he shall have whatsoever he saith" (Mark 11:23).

On the third day of redemption week, the sight of the withered fig tree led to an instructive lesson on faith in God, the Lord Jesus assuring the disciples that real faith could even move mountains into the sea. In parallel, on the third day of creation week, He had literally called the mountains up out of the sea (Gen. 1:9–10)!

It was also on this day that the Lord had to severely rebuke the Pharisees and Sadducees, beginning with two parables about a vineyard (Matt. 21:28–43). He reminded them that they had been placed in charge of God's vineyard on the earth, and had failed. Like the fig tree, there was no fruit for God from their service, and they must be removed.

Likewise, on day three of creation, the entire earth had been prepared as a beautiful garden, with an abundance of fruit to nourish every living creature (Gen. 1:11–12). It has been placed in man's care (Gen. 1:28–30; 2:15), but he has failed. Before the earth can become a beautiful garden again (Rev. 22:2), it must be purged, and the faithless keepers of the vineyard banished.

This third day of Passion Week was climaxed with His great discourse on the Mount of Olives, in which the Lord promised He would come again some day in power and great glory (Matt. 24). It was appropriate that He should then spend the night with His disciples there on the mountain, for the mount would call to memory that far-off third day of creation week when He had drawn all the mountains out of the sea. Also, the little Garden of Gethsemane — on its slope — would bring to mind the beautiful Garden of Eden and the verdant world He had planted everywhere that same day. Now, because of what He was about to accomplish in Jerusalem, the ground would some day be cleansed of its Curse and the world made new again.

THE LIGHTS
OF THE WORLD

"And God made two great lights; the greater light to rule the day, and the lesser light to rule the night. He made the stars also" (Gen. 1:16).

On the fourth day of creation week, the Lord Jesus had formed the sun and the moon and all the stars of heaven. There had been "light" on the first three days, but now there were actual *lights!* Not only would the earth and its verdure be a source of beauty and sustenance to man, but even the very heavens would bring joy and inspiration to him. Furthermore, they would guide his way, and keep his time.

But instead of the stars of heaven turning man's thoughts and affections toward His Creator, they had been corrupted and identified with a host of false gods and goddesses. Furthermore, instead of creating a sense of awe and reverence for the majesty of the One who could fill all heavens, they had bolstered the humanistic belief that the earth is insignificant and meaningless in such a vast, evolving cosmos. Perhaps thoughts such as these troubled the mind of the Lord that night as He lay on the mountain gazing at the lights He had long ago made for the darkness.

When morning came and day four of redemption week began, He returned to Jerusalem, where many were waiting to hear Him. He taught in the temple (Luke 21:37–38), but the synoptic gospels do not record His teachings. This lack is probably supplied in the apparently parenthetical record of His temple teaching as given only in the fourth Gospel (John 12:20–50), because there He twice compared himself to the lights He had made. "I am come a light into the world, that whosoever believeth on me should not abide in darkness." "Yet a little while is the light with you. Walk while ye have the light, lest darkness come upon you" (John 12:46, 35). He who was the true light must become darkness, in order that, in the new world, there would never be night again (Rev. 22:5). The sun and moon and stars which He had made would shine forever (Ps. 148:3–6), but in the New Jerusalem itself there would be no need for them, for "the Lamb is the light thereof" (Rev. 21:23).

THE LAMB
OF GOD

"Purge out therefore the old leaven, that ye may be a new lump, as ye are unleavened. For even Christ our passover is sacrificed for us" (1 Corinthians 5:7).

The fifth day of redemption week was the annual day for the Passover supper, so the Lord Jesus instructed two of His disciples to make preparations for their own observance of the feast that night (Mark 14:12–17). This is all that we know of His words during that day, but perhaps this scriptural silence is for the purpose of emphasizing the greater importance of these preparations for the Passover.

Multitudes of sacrificial lambs and other animals had been slain and their blood spilled through the centuries, but this would be the last such acceptable sacrifice. On the morrow, the Lamb of God would take away the sin of the world (John 1:29). He would offer one sacrifice for sins forever (Heb. 10:12). With the blood of His cross, He would become the great peacemaker, reconciling all things unto the Maker of those things (Col. 1:16, 20).

As the Lord thought about the shedding of the blood of that last Passover Lamb on that fifth day of Holy Week, He must also have thought of the fifth day of creation week, when He had first created all the animals. "God created . . . every living creature [Hebrew *nephesh*] that moveth" (Gen. 1:21). This had been His second great act of creation — this creation of the entity of conscious animal life (the first act of *ex nihilo* creation had been the creation of the physical elements, as recorded in Genesis 1:1). In these living animals, the "life" of the flesh was in their blood, and it was the blood which would later be accepted as an atonement for sin (Lev. 17:11). Note that the words "creature," "soul," and "life" are all translations of the same Hebrew word *nephesh*. Surely the shedding of the innocent blood of the lamb that day would recall the far-off day when the "life" in that blood had first been created. Because He, the Lamb of God, was about to become our Passover (note our text for the day), death itself would soon be gone (1 Cor. 15:54).

THE GROANING CREATION

"For we know that the whole creation groaneth and travaileth in pain together until now" (Rom. 8:22).

On the sixth day, man had been created in the image and likeness of God, the very climax and goal of God's great work of creation (Gen. 1:26–27). On *this* sixth day, God, made in the likeness of man, finished the even greater work of redemption.

Under the great Curse, the whole creation had long been groaning and travailing in pain. Now, the Creator himself had been made the Curse (Gal. 3:13; Isa. 52:14), and it seemed as though the creation also must die. Though He had made heaven and earth on the first day, now He had been lifted up from the earth (John 3:14) and the heavens were silent (Matt. 27:46). Though He had made the waters on the second day, He who was the very water of life (John 4:14), was dying of thirst (John 19:28).

On the third day, He had made the dry land, but now the "earth did quake, and the rocks rent" (Matt. 27:51) because the rock of salvation had been smitten (Exod. 17:6). He had also covered the earth with trees and vines on that third day, but now the true vine (John 15:1) had been plucked up and the green tree (Luke 23:31) cut down. He had made the sun on the fourth day, but now the sun was darkened (Luke 23:45) and the Light of the World (John 8:12) was burning out. On the fifth day, He had created life, and He, himself, *was* life (John 11:25; 14:6), but now the life of His flesh, the precious blood, was being poured out on the ground beneath the cross, and He had been brought into the "dust of death" (Ps. 22:15). On the sixth day, He had created man and given him life, but now man had despised the love of God and lifted up the Son of Man to death.

The creation has been groaning and travailing in pain ever since Adam's sin, but its Creator has paid the price for its redemption, and therefore, it will someday "be delivered from the bondage of corruption into the glorious liberty of the children of God" (Rom. 8:21). Because of what took place that day on the old, cursed earth, it will be made new on a great future day, and "there shall be no more curse" (Rev. 22:3).

CHRIST OUR PASSOVER

"And the blood shall be to you for a token upon the houses where ye are: and when I see the blood, I will pass over you, and the plague shall not be upon you to destroy you, when I smite the land of Egypt" (Exod. 12:13).

The Jews of the world have been keeping their annual Feast of the Passover for almost 3,500 years, fulfilling the ancient prophecy: "And ye shall observe this thing for an ordinance to thee and to thy sons for ever" (Exod. 12:24). This was the beginning of the nation of Israel, when they left Egyptian slavery behind and started their trek to the Promised Land. The lamb had been slain and eaten, its blood placed on the door posts, and the Lord had spared all their firstborn sons when the destroyer passed through the land of Egypt.

The feast was intended not only to memorialize the ancient deliverance, but also to anticipate the coming day when the "Lamb of God" would "take away the sin of the world" (John 1:29). The night before Christ was crucified, He told His disciples, "With desire I have desired to eat this passover with you before I suffer: For I say unto you, I will not any more eat thereof, until it be fulfilled in the kingdom of God" (Luke 22:15–16).

Thereupon, the Lord established His supper, which Christians will continue to observe to "show the Lord's death till He come" (1 Cor. 11:26). He fulfilled all that the Passover prophesied when He shed His blood on the Cross, "For even Christ our passover is sacrificed for us: Therefore let us keep the feast . . . with . . . sincerity and truth" (1 Cor. 5:7–8).

Now we look forward to an even greater supper when Christ returns, for the promise is this to all who believe: "Blessed are they which are called unto the marriage supper of the Lamb" (Rev. 19:9).

THE CUP
OF THE LORD

"Ye cannot drink the cup of the Lord, and the cup of devils: ye cannot be partakers of the Lord's table, and of the table of devils" (1 Cor. 10:21).

The "cup" is often used in the Bible as a figure of speech denoting some important spiritual doctrine. For example, there is the cup of sin and wickedness. "Ye make clean the outside of the cup and of the platter," Jesus told the hypocrites, "but within they are full of extortion and excess" (Matt. 23:25). Religious Babylon, the false church, is said to have "a golden cup in her hand full of abominations and filthiness of her fornication" (Rev. 17:4).

God, however, has a cup of wrath. "For in the hand of the LORD there is a cup, and the wine is red; it is full of mixture; and he poureth out of the same: but the dregs thereof, all the wicked of the earth shall wring them out, and drink them" (Ps. 75:8). "The same shall drink of the wine of the wrath of God, which is poured out without mixture into the cup of His indignation" (Rev. 14:10).

Yet, in His grace, His cup of wrath became the cup of His own sufferings, as He drank the cup in substitution for those who deserved it. "The cup which my Father hath given me, shall I not drink it?" (John 18:11). "This cup is the New Testament in my blood, which is shed for you" (Luke 22:20).

Our own cup thereby becomes a glorious cup, imparting everlasting life. "I will take the cup of salvation, and call upon the name of the LORD" (Ps. 116:13). We can then testify, "My cup runneth over. Surely goodness and mercy shall follow me all the days of my life: and I will dwell in the house of the LORD for ever" (Ps. 23:5–6).

At the Lord's table, as we remember His shed blood and broken body, we should reflect on all the cup symbolizes. "For as often as ye eat this bread, and drink this cup, ye do shew the Lord's death till he come" (1 Cor. 11:26).

MAN OF SORROWS

"He is despised and rejected of men; a man of sorrows, and acquainted with grief: and we hid as it were our faces from him; he was despised, and we esteemed him not" (Isa. 53:3).

"Man of sorrows!" What a name for the great Creator who came as man to be our Savior! Instead of being eagerly accepted by His creatures, He was rejected. We "esteemed him not" — that is, we "estimated him as nothing."

These heart-breaking words one day will become the confession of the nation of Israel (note Zech. 12:9–13:1), but they apply equally well to each of us today. This marvelous 53rd chapter of Isaiah is one of the greatest portions of the Bible, containing the most incisive and complete exposition of the doctrine of Christ's substitutionary atonement to be found anywhere. Isaiah 53 is an amazing prophecy, fulfilled in precise detail over 700 years after it was written.

"He was wounded for our transgressions, He was bruised for our iniquities" (verse 5). The word for "wounded" means "thrust through," referring to the savage spear thrust into His side. The word for "bruised" means "crushed and ground into the dust." He was "so marred more than any man" (Isa. 52:14). The "chastisement" and "stripes" (Isa. 53:5) anticipate the cruel scourgings He would receive from the Roman cat-o-nine-tails.

He was completely innocent, yet "He opened not His mouth" with complaint (verse 7). "The LORD hath laid on him the iniquity of us all" (verse 6) — that is, "laid on violently, with a death-dealing blow."

Psalm 22 also describes, in even more detail, the terrible sufferings of Christ both before and during His crucifixion — yet it was written before that form of execution was used. Most of all, however, Isaiah 53 emphasizes that it *was for us* that He suffered. "He shall see of the travail of his soul, and shall be satisfied . . . for he shall bear their iniquities" (Isa. 53:11).

CHRIST CAME
TO DIE

"And while they abode in Galilee, Jesus said unto them, The Son of man shall be betrayed into the hands of men: And they shall kill him, and the third day he shall be raised again. And they were exceeding sorry" (Matt. 17:22–23).

The death of the Lord Jesus was planned by Him and His Heavenly Father before the world began. Though His death took the disciples by surprise, Jesus had frequently told them that it was coming. Even as the soldiers were arresting Him, He said, "Thinkest thou that I cannot now pray to my Father, and He shall presently give me more than twelve legions of angels? But how then shall the scriptures be fulfilled, that thus it must be?" (Matt. 26:53–54).

The wondrous truth is that He did this for us! He was "delivered for our offences, and was raised again for our justification" (Rom. 4:25). The sad truth is that most people either doubt this great truth or ignore it or explain it away, and thus are yet unsaved. Many have not yet heard and they also are lost. Multitudes are following false religions. The followers of Mohammed, for example (over a billion of them), if they believe the Koran, believe that Jesus did not die at all, and thus they also are still under the guilt of their own sins. So are the Buddhists and Animists and Hindus and even "Christians" who have not personally trusted Christ as their redeeming Savior, for He himself said, "No man cometh unto the Father, but by me" (John 14:6). He also said: "Him that cometh to me I will in no wise cast out" (John 6:37).

We who do have the joy of truly knowing Christ as Savior and Lord have the responsibility and privilege of sharing the love of Christ with those who do not. We must get the good news to them in whatever way we can; that the Lord Jesus loves them and died for them too, and that "whosoever will may come."

CHRIST
OUR SIN-BEARER

"For such an high priest became us, who is holy, harmless, undefiled, separate from sinners, and made higher than the heavens; Who needeth not daily, as those high priests, to offer up sacrifice, first for his own sins, and then for the people's: for this he did once, when he offered up himself" (Heb. 7:26–27).

Again and again we are told two things in Scripture: first, that Jesus Christ was without sin of His own; second, that He died in substitution for the penalty of our sins. He was utterly "separate from sinners," yet "He offered up himself" to die for our sins.

It is clear that He *"did no sin,"* but then He "bare our sins in His own body on the tree" (1 Pet. 2:22, 24). Nor did He have a sin nature, for *"in him is no sin"* (1 John 3:5). Further, He *"knew no sin,"* yet God "hath made him to be sin for us" (2 Cor. 5:21). He *did* no sin, *knew* no sin, and *had* no sin, but He was *made* sin, and *bore* our sins!

"Christ also hath once suffered for sins, the just for the unjust, that he might bring us to God" (1 Pet. 3:18). "For as by one man's disobedience many were made sinners, so by the obedience of one shall many be made righteous" (Rom. 5:19). In many ways, these great themes appear time after time in the New Testament. Here is another: "Ye were not redeemed with corruptible things, as silver and gold. . . . But with the precious blood of Christ, as of a lamb without blemish and without spot" (1 Pet. 1:18–19).

Yet it is in the Old Testament (Isa. 52:13–53:12) that we find the fullest exposition of this incomparable truth. For example: "He had done no violence, neither was any deceit in his mouth. Yet it pleased the Lord to . . . make his soul an offering for sin. . . . My righteous servant [shall] justify many; for he shall bear their iniquities" (Isa. 53:9–11). Therefore, since He died for us, we should live for Him.

GAMBLING
AT CALVARY

"They part my garments among them, and cast lots upon my vesture"
(Ps. 22:18).

The Twenty-second Psalm is justly famous as a remarkable prophetic preview of the sufferings and death of the Lord Jesus on the cross, written by David approximately 1,000 years before it was fulfilled. It describes in accurate detail the sufferings of the Lord, and the actions of the sneering spectators as they watched Him die.

One of the most heartless acts of the Roman soldiers carrying out the crucifixion was the indignity of stripping Him of the garments He was wearing and then dividing them among themselves, even gambling to determine who would get His seamless vesture. The significance of this cruel scene is indicated by the fact that it is one of the very few specific events in the life of Christ recorded in all four Gospels.

We must not forget that the Lord Jesus Christ once had been arrayed, as it were, in beautiful garments that "smell of myrrh, and aloes, and cassia, out of the ivory palaces" (Ps. 45:8). He who was "equal with God" chose to be "made in the likeness of men" that He might eventually suffer "even the death of the cross" (Phil. 2:6–8) in order to save our unworthy souls. "For ye know the grace of our Lord Jesus Christ, that, though he was rich, yet for your sakes he became poor, that ye through his poverty might be rich" (2 Cor. 8:9).

He who had created the heavens, when He came to earth, had to say that "the Son of man hath not where to lay his head" (Matt. 8:20). His few remaining possessions were scavenged by His executioners as He died. Yet through His great sacrifice, He has provided "everlasting habitations" for us (Luke 16:9) and "all spiritual blessings in heavenly places" (Eph. 1:3). Indeed, we *do* know the grace of our Lord Jesus Christ!

JOSEPH
OF ARIMATHAEA

"Joseph of Arimathaea, an honorable counselor, which also waited for the kingdom of God, came, and went in boldly unto Pilate, and craved the body of Jesus" (Mark 15:43).

The unique service of Joseph, in giving Jesus an honorable burial after His execution as a criminal, is noted in all four gospels. He was a disciple of Jesus, as well as a rich man (Matt. 27:57). Although his home was in Arimathaea, he buried Jesus "in his own new tomb, which he had hewn out in the rock" (Matt. 27:60) on the side of Mount Calvary just outside Jerusalem — evidently built specifically for Jesus. Joseph "was a good man, and a just" man — a member of the Sanhedrin, who "had not consented to the counsel and deed of them" as they condemned Jesus to die (Luke 23:50–51).

These actions of Joseph soon would cost him his riches and his position. The same was true of his colleague on the council, Nicodemus, who had also become a disciple of Jesus, and who worked together with Joseph to plan the burial of their Lord, "secretly for fear of the Jews" (John 19:38). Once Christ had died, Joseph went to Pilate to request the body — so quickly that "Pilate marveled if He were already dead" (Mark 15:44). After checking this, "he gave the body to Joseph" (verse 45), and the two friends proceeded to prepare it for burial.

Nicodemus "brought a mixture of myrrh and aloes, about an hundred pound weight" (John 19:39), evidently from a cache in the tomb, and they wound Jesus' body in linen clothes with the spices and quickly buried Him, before sundown.

This loving ministry was performed to fulfill an ancient prophecy: "He made His grave . . . with the rich in His death" (Isa. 53:9). Somehow, Joseph and Nicodemus realized that God had called them to play this particular role in its fulfillment, enabling Jesus' body to rest in dignity until that morning when "He shall prolong his days, and the pleasure of the LORD shall prosper in his hand" (verse 10).

THE REMARKABLE MINISTRY
OF NICODEMUS

"There was a man of the Pharisees, named Nicodemus, a ruler of the Jews" (John 3:1).

The man named Nicodemus appears only on three occasions in the New Testament, but these three reveal a most remarkable character. In a way, he has become a "type" of all those who come to Christ for salvation. This was not easy for him, both because he was a member of the Pharisees who vigorously opposed Jesus, and also because he was a member of the Sanhedrin, the governing council which would eventually vote to have Jesus executed.

First, Nicodemus was an *interested inquirer,* coming to seek an understanding of Jesus and His mission. Similarly, those who come to Christ today must come with an open mind and heart, willing to take the time to learn of Christ and of their own need of salvation.

The Lord told Nicodemus his need of regeneration and then of God's gift of eternal life to those who would receive Christ and His sacrificial death. Nicodemus evidently believed, for we next see Him as *a confessing convert,* defending Christ in the midst of his own peers as they were seeking to arrest and imprison Him. "Nicodemus saith unto them. . . . Doth our law judge any man, before it hear him, and know what he doeth?" (John 7:50–51). This was perhaps a weak defense, but Nicodemus was a new convert, and even this stand was resented, and identified him with Christ in the minds of these powerful adversaries.

Finally, we see him as *a devoted disciple,* along with his friend Joseph, who also was on the council, willing to suffer the loss of position and riches for Christ's sake — for this is undoubtedly what their actions at the cross entailed. "And there came also Nicodemus. . . . and brought a mixture of myrrh and aloes, about an hundred pound weight. Then took they the body of Jesus. . . . for the sepulcher was nigh at hand" (John 19:39–42).

THE FORSAKEN ONE

"And about the ninth hour Jesus cried with a loud voice, saying, Eli, Eli, lama sabachthani? that is to say, My God, my God, why hast thou forsaken me?" (Matt. 27:46).

This is the central word of the seven "words" of Christ on the cross, this desolate cry at the very apex of His awful sufferings. As the Lamb of God was there being sacrificed for the sin of the world, it was fitting that all this should occur at the ninth hour, for this was the time of the regular evening sacrifice, as well as the time of evening prayers, among the people of ancient Israel.

It was at this hour that Elijah prayed to God against the prophets of Baal on Mount Carmel, and God answered by fire from heaven (1 Kings 18:36–39). This was also the hour of Ezra's great prayer of confession and intercession (Ezra 9:5), followed by a wonderful revival among the backslidden people of Israel. When Daniel uttered his own prayer of confession and intercession "about the time of the evening oblation" (Dan. 9:21), God sent the angel Gabriel to answer his prayer. In the New Testament, "Peter and John went up together into the temple at the hour of prayer, being the ninth hour" (Acts 3:1), and the result was the first apostolic miracle and Peter's great sermon at the Beautiful Gate of the temple. The first Gentile convert to Christ was Cornelius, who was praying "about the ninth hour of the day" (Acts 10:3) when he, like Daniel, received a visit from an angel of God to tell him to send for Peter, who would lead him to Christ.

In all such recorded instances of prayer at the ninth hour, the hour of the daily evening sacrifice, God answered the prayer in a marvelous way. When the Lord Jesus Christ prayed, God did *not* answer, for He had forsaken His own Son.

"Why?" was the central word in the central "Word" spoken by Christ. He did not cry because of the terrible physical sufferings, but because of the far more terrible spiritual desolation, as He endured the agonies of hell itself. The answer to the awful question is simply that He "loved me, and gave himself for me." The measure of His love is the cross and separation from the Father, "that he by the grace of God should taste death for every man" (Heb. 2.9).

WE CAN NEVER REALLY comprehend the terrible sufferings of Christ when He died to pay the price of redemption, covering all the sins of all people of all time, but each of us can simply believe and be grateful that He included "me." To think that Jesus Christ "loved me, and gave himself for me" (Gal. 2:20)! The greatest sin one could ever commit — the one unforgivable sin, in fact — is to reject or ignore this "unspeakable gift" (2 Cor. 9:15).

THE AWFUL CRY
FROM THE CROSS

"My God, my God, why hast thou forsaken me? why art thou so far from helping me, and from the words of my roaring?" (Ps. 22:1).

This is the first verse in Psalm 22, surely one of the most remarkable prophetic chapters ever penned, describing in detail the awful sufferings of Christ on the cross a thousand years before it happened. The verse itself is the heart-rending cry of the Lord Jesus during the terrible supernatural darkness when even His Heavenly Father had turned His back on Him. Why could such a thing be, when He had always been "holy, harmless, undefiled, separate from sinners" even though He had been "in all points tempted [or, more accurately, 'tested'] like as we are" (Heb. 7:26; 4:15).

The reason why is because His Father had "made him to be sin for us, who knew no sin; that we might be made the righteousness of God in him" (2 Cor. 5:21), and God in His essential nature is "of purer eyes than to behold evil, and canst not look on iniquity" (Hab. 1:13). His beloved only begotten Son had willingly allowed himself to be offered as the sacrificial "Lamb of God, which taketh away the sin of the world" (John 1:29). Although He was neither "roaring" nor "moaning" outwardly, He was indeed *roaring* inwardly (compare Ps. 32:3) with the infinite weight of all the world's sin on His soul.

What an amazing transaction — He suffered and died for our sins so that we could be set free to enjoy the fruits of His perfect righteousness eternally! Now we can say with Paul: "I live by the faith of the Son of God, who loved me, and gave himself for me" (Gal. 2:20). We live for Him, who died for us! "For the love of Christ constraineth us . . . that they which live should not henceforth live unto themselves, but unto him which died for them, and rose again" (2 Cor. 5:14–15).

It Is
Finished!

*"When Jesus therefore had received the vinegar, he said, It is finished:
and he bowed his head, and gave up the ghost"* (John 19:30).

O n the seventh day God ended his work which he had made" (Gen.
2:2). Furthermore, "every thing that he had made . . . was very
good" (Gen. 1:31).

So is His work of salvation! Jesus, knowing that all things were now
accomplished, that the Scripture might be *fulfilled*, said, It is *finished*. (John
19:28, 30). The emphasized words ("accomplished," "fulfilled," "finished")
are all the same in the Greek original.

When all the relevant Scriptures had been fulfilled and the price of
reconciliation ("the blood of his cross," Col. 1:20) fully paid, He could
finally shout the great victory cry (Matt. 27:50), "*It is finished!*" As the
finished creation was "very good," so is our finished salvation. The salvation which Christ our Creator thus provided on the cross is "so great"
(Heb. 2:3) and "eternal" (Heb. 5:9), that the hope thereof is "good"
(2 Thess. 2:16).

Then, finally, having finished the work of redemption, Christ *rested
once again*, on the seventh day. As He had rested on that first seventh day,
now He could rest again, His body sleeping in Joseph's tomb.

He had died quickly, and the preparations for burial had been hurried
(Luke 23:54–56), so that He could be buried before the Sabbath. On the
third day (that is, the first day of the new week), He would rise again, as He
had said (Matt. 16:21, et al.). His body rested in the tomb all the Sabbath
Day, plus part of the previous and following days, according to Hebrew
idiomatic usage, "three days and three nights" (Matt. 12:40) — but death
could hold Him no longer. He arose from the dead and is now "alive for
evermore" (Rev. 1:18).

THE DAY
OF GOD'S REST

"For in six days the LORD made heaven and earth, the sea, and all that in them is, and rested the seventh day: wherefore the LORD blessed the sabbath day, and hallowed it" (Exod. 20:11).

God's Word is omnipotent, and He could just as well have created an entire universe, fully populated and functioning, in an instant of time. Instead, He chose to do it in six days, with a seventh day to be set aside as a day of rest and remembrance of His completed, very good, creation. Since that time, although a certain amount of disagreement has arisen concerning *which* day of the week should be regarded as this special day, it has been the universal practice among monotheists, those who believe in one Creator God, to measure time in seven-day weeks, with one of those days observed as a day of rest and worship of the Creator. Many years later, that same Creator would rest on another Sabbath Day — this time in an earthly tomb, when He had also finished His completed, very good work of redemption!

This divine assertion was inscribed with "the finger of God" on a table of stone (Exod. 31:18), clearly settling once and for all the ancient question of the age of the cosmos, at least for those who really believe in the inerrant perspicuity and authority of the Holy Scriptures. Not only did the Lord precisely equate the six days of man's work week with the six days of His own work week, but He then pronounced it all "very good" and "sanctified" the seventh (i.e., "sabbath") day (Gen. 1:31; 2:3). This would have been an unthinkable thing for Him to say if there were, at that time, a great mile-deep graveyard, consisting of the fossil remains of dead animals from the so-called geological ages, extending all around the globe. These fossils must all be dated as post-Eden, after sin brought death into the world (Rom. 5:12).

In the meantime, those who still believe in God and creation should certainly continue to remember Him by observing every seventh day as a day of rest and worship, in honor of their Creator, who has now also become their Redeemer and will soon come again to reign as eternal King.

THE FINISHED
WORKS OF GOD

"Thus the heavens and the earth were finished, and all the host of them. And on the seventh day God ended his work which he had made; and he rested on the seventh day from all his work which he had made" (Gen. 2:1–2).

At the end of the six work days of creation week, God rested on the seventh day, blessing and sanctifying it. "In six days the LORD made heaven and earth, the sea, and all that in them is, and rested the seventh day" (Exod. 20:11).

This testimony of a finished creation, with nothing further to be created, completely repudiates the humanistic philosophy of evolution, according to which, the supposed laws of nature are still "creating" new kinds of organisms, as well as new stars and new planets.

There is also another vital work of God — the work of redemption. As soon as man sinned, God began the long process of preparing the world for the coming of the Savior to pay the price for man's redemption. "When the fullness of the time was come" (Gal. 4:4), God entered the realm of human life, becoming a man, in order to die for the sins of all men. Finally, as He hung on the cross, having fulfilled every prophecy and endured the full wrath of God against human sin, He shouted the great shout of victory: "It is finished" (John 19:30). As He had once finished the great work of creation, He now had finished the greater work of redemption. The Lord Jesus Christ is both Creator and Redeemer.

Then He sealed and settled it by His resurrection. What, then, is there left for us to do? Nothing! Just as there is nothing God's finished creation can do to evolve itself higher, so there is nothing God's redeemed creation can do to finish paying the price for its salvation.

The only thing we can do is to receive what He has done, with gratitude. We can believe in Him as Creator and Savior. Then, we can love Him and live for Him, forever.

THE SPIRITS
IN PRISON

"For Christ also hath once suffered for sins, the just for the unjust, that he might bring us to God, being put to death in the flesh, but quickened by the Spirit: By which also he went and preached unto the spirits in prison" (1 Pet. 3:18–19).

Just who were these imprisoned spirits to whom Christ preached when He had been "put to death in the flesh"? This has been a controversial verse, so one should not be dogmatic in discussing it. However, the idea that these were souls in purgatory to whom Christ was offering a second chance is clearly wrong, for Hebrews 9:27 declares plainly that "it is appointed unto men once to die, but after this the judgment."

One point often overlooked is that the word "spirits" can apply to angels as well as human beings. In fact, when it occurs in the plural, as it does here, it refers specifically to angels in at least 26 of its 30 occurrences.

This strongly suggests that these were evil spirits to whom Christ was (literally) "proclaiming" the victory He had won over Satan when He had "once suffered for sins" on the Cross (the same word is translated "proclaimed" in Luke 12:3 — "proclaimed upon the housetops"). These fallen angels had tried to corrupt all flesh "in the days of Noah" (1 Pet. 3:20; see Gen. 6:1–4, 12), and therefore had been cast "down to hell" and "delivered them into chains of darkness, to be reserved unto judgment" (2 Pet. 2:4).

As Peter had preached on the day of Pentecost: "His soul was not left in hell. . . . This Jesus hath God raised up" and "hath made that same Jesus, whom ye have crucified, both Lord and Christ" (Acts 2:31–32, 36). Thus, He is now our Lord Jesus Christ, to whom some day soon "every knee should bow . . . in heaven, and . . . in earth, and . . . under the earth" (Phil. 2:10).

He Shall Prolong His Days

*"Yet it pleased the L*ORD *to bruise him; he hath put him to grief: when thou shalt make his soul an offering for sin, he shall see his seed, he shall prolong his days, and the pleasure of the L*ORD *shall prosper in his hand"* (Isa. 53:10).

In this one verse, found in the wonderful 53rd chapter of Isaiah, there is an amazing prophecy of the sacrificial death of the Lord Jesus Christ in atonement for our sins, His resurrection from the dead, and the resulting salvation of many lost sinners.

This Old Testament chapter, written 600 years before Christ, contains probably the most complete and cogent exposition of the saving work of Christ on the cross to be found in the entire Bible.

How could it "please" the Lord to bruise His only begotten Son? It could only be because of His love for those He had created and the great work this would accomplish.

Then, indeed, "the pleasure of the Lord" would be realized. As to the Son, "He shall see of the travail of his soul, and shall be satisfied" (Isa. 53:10–11).

After the Father has allowed the enemies of His Son to "bruise him" to death, it would be soon known that this was actually "an offering for sin" and that, having satisfied the requirements of God's holiness, the Son "shall prolong his days." Though He died and actually "made his grave with the wicked, and with the rich in his death" (verse 9), death could not hold Him, and "he shall prolong his days." As He would later proclaim: "I am alive for evermore" (Rev. 1:18).

Because He has done this, He "shall see his seed." "For it became him, for whom are all things, and by whom are all things, in bringing many sons unto glory, to make the captain of their salvation perfect through sufferings" (Heb. 2:10). What a wonderful Savior!

MANY
INFALLIBLE PROOFS

"To whom also he shewed himself alive after his passion by many infallible proofs, being seen of them forty days, and speaking of the things pertaining to the kingdom of God" (Acts 1:3).

Jesus Christ is both Creator and Savior and, just as the miracle of special creation is the most certain testimony of true science, so the miracle of His bodily resurrection is the most certain testimony of true history.

There is, first of all, the witness of the empty tomb. When John first entered the tomb and observed the linen clothes and the napkin for His head collapsed inwardly on themselves, with the body gone, "he saw, and believed" (John 20:6–8). Though they surely would have if they could have, neither the Jews nor the Romans could stop the spreading flame of Christianity by producing His dead body, for that body was alive again and soon ascended to heaven, far beyond their reach.

Then there were at least ten appearances of the resurrected Savior to one or more of the disciples. Paul recounts some: "He was seen of Cephas, then of the twelve: After that, he was seen of about five hundred brethren at once; of whom the greater part remain unto this present. . . . After that, he was seen of James; then of all the apostles. And last of all he was seen of me also" (1 Cor. 15:5–8). These appearances were neither of a ghost nor hallucinations, for He had "flesh and bones" (Luke 24:39); they touched Him and talked with Him and ate with Him.

These, and many other "infallible proofs," so convinced them and multitudes of others, that their lives were transformed, and they became willing to live and even to die for Him. They suffered severely for their faith and had every incentive to assess the evidence critically, yet not one recanted. "The Lord is risen indeed" (Luke 24:34), and we certainly "have not followed cunningly devised fables" (2 Pet. 1:16).

AMONG THE "many infallible proofs" (Acts 1:3) of Christ's resurrection was the unshakeable testimony of the women who were the first at the tomb on that resurrection morning. They found that the guards had fled, the great stone had been "rolled away from the sepulcher," the body was gone, and two men "in shining garments" were there telling them that Jesus was alive (Luke 24:1–7).

WITNESSES OF
THE RESURRECTION

"Wherefore of these men which have companied with us all the time that the Lord Jesus went in and out among us, Beginning from the baptism of John, unto that same day that he was taken up from us, must one be ordained to be a witness with us of his resurrection" (Acts 1:21–22).

The most important event since the creation itself was the resurrection of Christ, and it was vital that the witness of His chosen apostles focus especially on this great event. They must believe with confidence in His bodily resurrection, having been with Him throughout His ministry, heard His predictions of the resurrection, then seen the infallible proofs thereof, especially the empty tomb and His post-resurrection appearances. Both the original 11 and Matthias, chosen to replace Judas, satisfied these requirements.

Then after the coming of God's Holy Spirit at Pentecost, "with great power gave the apostles witness of the resurrection . . . and great grace was upon them all" (Acts 4:33). The resurrection proved that Christ was the Creator and Savior, for only the Creator of life could defeat death.

Paul also saw the risen Christ on the road to Damascus, and thus he also could be an apostle. "Am I not an apostle? . . . Have I not seen Jesus Christ our Lord?" he could say (1 Cor. 9:1). Only those who had seen the risen Lord and been specifically chosen by Him could be true apostles, for they must be credible witnesses of His resurrection.

That they were! Peter could say, "We are witnesses of all things which he did . . . whom they slew and hanged on a tree: Him God raised up" (Acts 10:39–40). Paul could say "God raised him from the dead: And he was seen many days of them . . . who are his witnesses" (Acts 13:30–31).

Yes, the apostles were true witnesses of Christ's resurrection, and multitudes have received eternal salvation because they were!

RAISED FOR OUR JUSTIFICATION

"Who was delivered for our offences, and was raised again for our justification" (Rom. 4:25).

We rejoice greatly in Christ's resurrection, knowing that He has promised that "because I live, ye shall live also" (John 14:19). It is also very important to realize and remember that if He had not been raised from the dead, we would still be lost sinners, separated eternally from God. He was raised, Paul reminds us, "for our justification."

The immensity of the load of sin which Christ bore with Him on the cross is beyond comprehension. He had to "taste death for every man" (Heb. 2:9), for He was the offering "for the sins of the whole world" (1 John 2:2). Since "the wages of sin is death" (Rom. 6:23), were it not for the infinite power, as well as the infinite love, of both the Father and the Son, such an infinite weight of sin would seem impossible to overcome, so Christ would die forever, and we would be lost forever. How could we ever know that we had been forgiven and that He had paid the awful price that would suffice for our salvation? How could we ever be acquitted, and declared righteous before God?

That is exactly what the resurrection of Christ assures! "By the righteousness of one the free gift came upon all men unto justification of life" (Rom. 5:18). His infinite righteousness has more than balanced the terrible weight of "the sin of the world," and He was able to take it away (John 1:29). Although the wages of sin must be death, "the free gift is of many offences unto justification" (Rom. 5:16).

This gift of total and eternal justification is free because of His love, but even a free gift must be accepted before it can be possessed. "Therefore being justified by faith, we have peace with God through our Lord Jesus Christ" (Rom. 5:1).

THE RISEN
PRINCE AND SAVIOR

"The God of our fathers raised up Jesus, whom ye slew and hanged on a tree. Him hath God exalted with his right hand to be a Prince and a Saviour, for to give repentance to Israel, and forgiveness of sins" (Acts 5:30–31).

This was the courageous response given by Peter and the apostles when the chief priests ordered them not to teach any more in the name of Christ. "We ought to obey God rather than men" they said (verse 29), and proceeded in effect to preach the gospel to the priests themselves!

The central theme of that gospel is the death of Christ "for the forgiveness of sins" as our "Saviour," and His bodily resurrection to be our "Prince." The Greek word for "Prince" (*archeogos*) is also used in Hebrews 2:10 and 12:2, where the Lord Jesus is called "the *captain* of their salvation" and "the *author . . .* of our faith," respectively.

He is indeed "King of kings and Lord of lords" to us, and will one day soon be acknowledged as such by all men and women of all nations and times (Phil. 2:9–11). No other famous religious founder and leader (Mohammed, Buddha, Confucius, etc.) was ever put to death for his teachings, and no other religious founder and leader ever rose from the grave, never to die again! Mohammed is still in his grave and so are Buddha and Confucius and all the rest.

Our Prince and Savior Jesus Christ has defeated death and is alive, in His glorified *physical* body at the right hand of the Father, where He "ever liveth to make intercession for [us]" (Heb. 7:25). It is sad that hundreds of millions of people around the world place their faith in the futile words of so-called teachers and prophets who could neither "give repentance" nor "forgiveness of sins" to anyone, while they ignore the One who can "save them to the uttermost that come unto God by him" (Heb. 7:25), and has proved it by His bodily resurrection from the dead.

THE KING
OF GLORY

"Who is this King of glory? The LORD of hosts, he is the King of glory. Selah" (Ps. 24:10).

In the Upper Room just before His betrayal, the Lord Jesus prayed to His Father, remembering "the glory which I had with thee before the world was" (John 17:5). He had left heaven, however, when "the Word was made flesh, and dwelt among us, (and we beheld His glory, the glory as of the only begotten of the Father,) full of grace and truth" (John 1:14). Then, when He miraculously turned water into wine at the wedding in Galilee, He "manifested forth his glory; and his disciples believed on him" (John 2:11).

In the days of His flesh, His glory was veiled, however, except in His life and words of grace and truth, and in His mighty works. He "made himself of no reputation, and took upon him the form of a servant, and was made in the likeness of men: And being found in fashion as a man, he humbled himself, and became obedient unto death, even the death of the cross" (Phil. 2:7–8).

Finally, His glory seemed to be gone forever as He lay dead in a borrowed tomb. Then "God . . . raised him up from the dead, and gave him glory; that your faith and hope might be in God" (1 Pet. 1:21).

He is now "the Lord of glory" (James 2:1), who, being the very "brightness of [God's] glory, and the express image of his person, and upholding all things by the word of his power, when he had by himself purged our sins, sat down on the right hand of the Majesty on high" (Heb. 1:3).

As He ascended back to heaven, all His hosts of angels welcomed their Lord of hosts with a mighty anthem of praise: "Lift up your heads, O ye gates; even lift them up, ye everlasting doors; and the King of glory shall come in. Who is this King of glory? The LORD of hosts, he is the King of glory" (Ps. 24:9–10).

TRULY THE
SON OF GOD

"He that believeth on him is not condemned: but he that believeth not is condemned already, because he hath not believed in the name of the only begotten Son of God" (John 3:18).

It is noteworthy that the identification of Jesus Christ as the Son of God is directly associated with His resurrection from the dead. Note Romans 1:4, "Declared to be the Son of God . . . by the resurrection from the dead." Since only God himself can conquer death, Christ's bodily resurrection is the conclusive affirmation of His unique Deity: "Thou art the Christ, the Son of the *living* God" (Matt. 16:16). Many others have claimed divine sonship, but all are dead — only Christ validated that claim by defeating death. "God . . . hath raised up Jesus again; as it is also written in the Second Psalm, Thou art my Son, this day have I begotten thee" (Acts 13:33). "Death is swallowed up in victory . . . through our Lord Jesus Christ" (1 Cor. 15:54–57).

Jesus is explicitly called "the Son of God" about 44 times in the New Testament, only half as often as He is called "Son of Man." Nevertheless, this great truth is clearly taught in numerous other ways than by the use of the title itself. It is so important that there is no salvation for the one who denies it. Jesus said plainly "He that believeth on him is not condemned, but, he that believeth not is condemned already, because he hath not believed in the name of the only begotten Son of God" (John 3:18).

Because He lives, we who believe on His name will also live — forever! "Who is he that overcometh the world, but he that believeth that Jesus is the Son of God?" "He that hath the Son hath life: and he that hath not the Son of God hath not life. These things have I written unto you that believe on the name of the Son of God; that ye may know that ye have eternal life" (1 John 5:5, 12–13).

THE GARDENS
OF THE LORD

"When Jesus had spoken these words, he went forth with his disciples over the brook Cedron, where was a garden, into the which he entered, and his disciples" (John 18:1).

As Jesus, after the last supper with His disciples, walked out with them, they soon crossed over a small brook and entered the little garden called Gethsemane. Eventually He left the disciples and went farther into the garden alone for a time of solitary prayer.

Perhaps He remembered how, long ago, He had walked in His first garden with Adam and Eve in beautiful fellowship. Then they had rebelled against His word, and had to be expelled from the Garden of Eden, leaving Him alone there also (Gen. 3:8).

As He prayed in Gethsemane, He knew that it would be only a few hours before He would be buried in still another garden, one "wherein was never man yet laid" (John 19:41). He would be carried to a new tomb prepared in a newly planted garden by the loving hands of Joseph and Nicodemus, but then He would be alone once again.

He had walked alone in the first garden, seeking His own; then had knelt alone in the second garden, praying for His own; and finally, was buried alone in the third garden, after dying for His own.

Because He came "to seek and to save that which was lost" (Luke 19:10), and because He now "ever liveth to make intercession for them" (Heb. 7:25), after paying the awful price of "redemption through his blood" (Eph. 1:7), all those who believe and trust Him will spend eternity in fellowship with Him in a beautiful garden city, where flows "a pure river of water of life" surrounded on both sides by "the tree of life, which bare twelve manner of fruits, and yielded her fruit every month" (Rev. 22:1–2), and all will be "very good" forever.

RESURRECTION AND CREATION

"And he is before all things, and by him all things consist. And he is the head of the body, the church: who is the beginning, the firstborn from the dead; that in all things he might have the preeminence" (Col. 1:17–18).

The two greatest miracles in all history were the creation of the world and the resurrection of its Creator. In our devotional studies, we have noted the remarkable parallels between the week of creation and the week of redemption, with both these incomparable work-weeks completed with a day of divine rest.

Then, that One who was "before all things" became also "the firstborn from the dead." Only the Creator could redeem His lost creation, cursed and dying because of sin, by himself taking the curse and dying for sin. God, however, cannot die (in the sense of ceasing to exist), for He is life itself. His mortal body could sleep in the grave, and His Holy Spirit suffer the anguish of hell, but it was inevitable that He must conquer sin and death. The omnipotent Creator cannot possibly fail in His purpose in creation. In all things, He *must* have the preeminence, for it is only by Him that things exist at all!

The two-fold testimony of the empty tomb and the post-Resurrection bodily appearances of Christ to His disciples, confirmed by their unshakeable witness (even unto death), and the inability of their opponents to exhibit His dead body (now risen from the tomb and inaccessible in heaven) assures us forever that "he is risen, as he said!" (Matt. 28:6).

Therefore, as creation is the foundation of all true science, so the Resurrection is the centrality of all true history. All real facts of science support the primeval creation, and the best-proved fact of real history is the Resurrection. As the great apostle preached long ago in the very center of all human culture in Athens, "God that made the world and all things therein, seeing that he is Lord of heaven and earth . . . hath appointed a day, in the which he will judge the world in righteousness by that man whom he hath ordained; whereof he hath given assurance unto all men, in that he hath raised him from the dead" (Acts 17:24–31).

Chapter III

THE NEW YEAR

The people of almost every nation observe some kind of New Year holiday. However, the actual date of the beginning of the year has varied widely in both time and nation. A number of ancient peoples began their year at the autumnal equinox (September 21), but the early Romans and Greeks began theirs at the winter solstice (December 21). The people of Israel have tended to follow two annual years — the civil year beginning on a varying date in September or early October, and the ecclesiastical year sometime around the spring equinox (March 21). Other religions have various and widely differing calendars.

The detailed history of the calendar is thus exceedingly complex and has little direct bearing on the common observances in Christendom today of the coming of our customary New Year's date. New Year's Eve has all too frequently degenerated here into a time of hilarity and relaxed morals, and then New Year's Day into a time of superficial repentance of the past and good resolutions for future behavior.

The significance of the date for the Christian is naturally not to be governed by worldly customs, but hopefully by serious concerns for one's Christian behavior and testimony before God and the world. These are the themes emphasized in the devotional Bible studies in this chapter.

LOADED
WITH BLESSING

"Blessed be the LORD, who daily loadeth us with benefits, even the God of our salvation. Selah" (Ps. 68:19).

As we come to the year's end, it is salutary for the believer to think back over the days of the year and to meditate upon his or her blessings. They may, indeed, have experienced defeats and losses, disappointments and injuries in great number. If they are honest with themselves, however, each Christian will always have to acknowledge that the blessings far outweigh the burdens. God has "loaded us with benefits," and is even working in and through all the trials and hurtful things together for our good (Rom. 8:28).

In our text verse, the words "with benefits" have been supplied by the translators. Some might, therefore, conclude that the verse could mean that God is daily loading us with burdens, instead of benefits. The context, however, assures us that the emphasis is really on His blessings. For that matter, even a burden can become a blessing, if we take it as a gift from God for our spiritual benefit.

Therefore: "Bless the LORD, O my soul, and forget not all his benefits" (Ps. 103:2). "In every thing give thanks: for this is the will of God in Christ Jesus concerning you" (1 Thess. 5:18). "Rejoice in the Lord alway: and again I say, Rejoice" (Phil. 4:4).

He has given us "life, and breath, and all things" (Acts 17:25). Far more importantly, He is "the God of our salvation." Whatever else we have, or don't have, in this life, we have the great gift of eternal life, through faith in Christ and His finished work of redemption. We have it every day of the year and are daily ready to meet the Lord, whenever He calls. Each day we have the indwelling presence of His Spirit, the illuminating guidance of His Word, the daily provision of all real needs, and the assurance of His love. He has surely loaded us with benefits!

A Year of Coronations

"Thou crownest the year with thy goodness; and thy paths drop fatness" (Ps. 65:11).

At year's end, a Christian believer should always stop to count his blessings of that year. If he does this honestly and fully, no matter what his problems and troubles may have been during the year, he will have to confess that God, as always, has crowned the year with goodness.

The coronation figure is frequently used in Scripture to speak of God's blessings in the Christian life. For example: "Who redeemeth thy life from destruction; who crowneth thee with lovingkindness and tender mercies" (Ps. 103:4). Even our testings and trials are always in the context of God's grace and love. Christ himself wore a crown of thorns so that we may be crowned with mercy and salvation.

Consider also Psalm 5:12: "For thou, LORD, will bless the righteous; with favor wilt thou compass him as with a shield." The word "compass" here is the same Hebrew word as "crown," the basic meaning being "encircle." We are surrounded and crowned with God's protecting favor. Other jewels in the year-end crown for the believer are God's grace and glory. "[Wisdom] shall give to thine head an ornament of grace: a crown of glory shall she deliver to thee" (Prov. 4:9).

Then there is the wonderful testimony of the Eighth Psalm: "For thou hast made him a little lower than the angels, and hast crowned him with glory and honor" (Ps. 8:5). Finally, the believer's crown is none other than the Lord himself: "In that day shall the LORD of hosts be for a crown of glory, and for a diadem of beauty, unto the residue of his people" (Isa. 28:5).

Most Christians also have an abundance of material blessings to count at the end of the year, for which to thank the Lord. Even if they have none of these, however, God has crowned the year with goodness and favor, with lovingkindness and tender mercies, with grace and glory and honor and, best of all, with His own presence. "Bless the LORD, O my soul, and forget not all his benefits" (Ps. 103:2).

HARVEST
IS PAST

"The harvest is past, the summer is ended, and we are not saved"
(Jer. 8:20).

This moving lament from the "weeping prophet" denotes the ending of another sad year in Judah's decline as the prophet is grieving over her still unrepentant state. God had issued repeated warnings through Jeremiah and other prophets, but it was almost to no avail, and now they were on the verge of being deported into Babylon as slaves and prisoners. Once they had been one of the greatest kingdoms in the world, but they had gone after the false gods of evolutionary pantheism and the corresponding idolatrous, immoral practices associated with this system, and now they were nearing the end, still unsaved.

God does not change, and one fears that "Christian" America is fast approaching similar rejection by the God who has blessed her so abundantly. At each year's end — despite all the blessings we still enjoy — the moral and spiritual condition of America, perhaps even of evangelical Christianity in America, seems to have plunged deeper than ever into the morass of compromise and open ridicule of God's truth and godly lifestyles.

God has been calling us to repentance through the preaching of the Word and various judgments (drugs, AIDS, etc.), but to no avail. The year is ended, and America is not saved! "The LORD's hand is not shortened, that it cannot save; neither his ear heavy, that it cannot hear: But your iniquities have separated between you and your God, and your sins have hid his face from you, that he will not hear" (Isa. 59:1–2).

The individual believer may not be able to change the face of America, but he should do what he can — thanking God for past blessings, confessing and repenting his own sins, doing all he can in his own sphere of influence to honor the Lord in all things.

GLORIFYING GOD

"Whoso offereth praise glorifieth me: and to him that ordereth his conversation aright will I shew the salvation of God" (Ps. 50:23).

The great summarizing commandment of the apostle Paul was: "Whether therefore ye eat, or drink, or whatsoever ye do, do all to the glory of God" (1 Cor. 10:31). That is, every aspect of our lives should be so ordered as to glorify God in whatever we say and do.

This is a difficult rule to follow, for how do we determine whether such and such an action glorifies God or not? Nevertheless, there is one thing we can do which we can be absolutely certain does glorify Him — that is, offering to Him our praise and thanks. We should offer praise for His person and work in general, and thanks for what He is and does for us in particular. "*Whoso offereth praise glorifieth me!*"

This is His assurance and our incentive to praise Him in all things. "In every thing give thanks," says the Apostle, "for this is the will of God in Christ Jesus concerning you" (1 Thess. 5:18).

On the last day of each year, especially, praise and thanks should pour from our hearts and lips, if we would "order our conversation aright." "Bless the LORD, O my soul," says the Psalmist, "and forget not all his benefits" (Ps. 103:2). Most of us all too commonly tend to forget all His benefits and fret over our troubles and burdens.

If we desire to glorify God, on the other hand, we should recount all our blessings and leave our burdens with Him. In the words of the old hymn: "Count your many blessings, see what God hath done!" Then will "the peace of God, which passeth all understanding" (Phil. 4:7) fill our hearts and minds, enabling the indwelling Holy Spirit to "shew the salvation of God" not only *to* us, but *in* us and *through* us to others.

GOD DOES INDEED SUPPLY all the needs of His loved ones (Phil. 4:19) as they ask and trust Him. It is a real blessing to have godly parents who will teach this great truth to their children, beginning when they are very young. And the New Year is a wonderful time to thank God for all His goodness to us in the past and to pray for guidance and provision for the future.

THE GREAT PROVIDER

"But my God shall supply all your need according to His riches in glory by Christ Jesus" (Phil. 4:19).

God is a wonderful provider. He provides the air and the rain and all the real necessities of life, even for those who don't believe in Him. The very life that all in their right minds seek desperately to keep going as long as possible has been given by God. As Paul reminded the pagan Greeks at Athens, "He giveth to all life, and breath, and all things" (Acts 17:25). He had previously reminded the pagans at Lystra that God in each nation "did good, and gave us rain from heaven, and fruitful seasons, filling our hearts with food and gladness" (Acts 14:17).

He even provides for the needs of the animals. "These wait all upon thee; that thou mayest give them their meat in due season" (Ps. 104:27). He cares about every little bird, for He created them too; "not one of them is forgotten before God" (Luke 12:6). He cares too for all the beasts of burden. "Thou shalt not muzzle the mouth of the ox that treadeth out the corn. Doth God take care for oxen?" (1 Cor. 9:9).

Yes, indeed, He does! If not one sparrow can "fall on the ground without your Father" (Matt. 10:29) and not one ox must ever be denied the food he needs to do his work, then we can be sure that God is concerned about you and me. "Your heavenly Father feedeth them. Are ye not much better than they?" (Matt. 6:26).

In other words, New Year's Eve should not be a time of revelry, but of thanksgiving, especially for any true, believing Christian. Like the lives of the martyrs, like that of Christ himself, there is suffering and sorrow in each of our lives here on earth, but if we are honest in our memories, there have been infinitely more blessings, year after year, so this should be a day of gratitude.

Remembering God, Our Help

"When I remember thee upon my bed, and meditate on thee in the night watches. Because thou hast been my help, therefore in the shadow of thy wings will I rejoice" (Ps. 63:6–7).

The 63rd Psalm was written by David when he was out in the wilderness at night and in grave danger from "those that seek my soul, to destroy it," yet he could confidently affirm that "the king shall rejoice in God" (Ps. 63:9, 11), for God had always been his help.

Is that not just as true today, for those who trust in God? New Year's Eve may be, for many at least, a time of merry-making and fun, but when the parties are over and we realize that the old year has really gone, and we fall into our beds, would that not be an especially fitting time to "meditate on thee in the night watches"? Whatever may have been the difficulties encountered in the year that has just passed, for the believing Christian, God has always been there to help, and the blessings of the year must also be taken into account. "Bless the LORD, O my soul, and forget not all his benefits" (Ps. 103:2).

Just to "meditate on thee," the wonderful plan of God for His redeemed in the ages to come, will turn distress into confidence and sorrow into rejoicing. "How precious also are thy thoughts unto me, O God! how great is the sum of them. If I should count them, they are more in number than the sand: when I awake, I am still with thee" (Ps. 139:17–18).

In another of his incomparable psalms, David could sing out joyfully: "Thou crownest the year with thy goodness" (Ps. 65:11). Can that not also be our testimony as every year ends? The same coronation word was also used by David in the matchless 103rd Psalm. God, the Psalmist sang, "redeemeth thy life from destruction; who crowneth thee with lovingkindness and tender mercies" (Ps. 103:4). So, "bless the LORD, O my soul" (Ps. 103:22).

THE LAND OF
FORGETFULNESS

"Shall thy wonders be known in the dark? and thy righteousness in the land of forgetfulness?" (Ps. 88:12).

Psalm 88 could be considered as the mournful lamentation of its author, Heman the Ezrahite, who suddenly felt his whole life of service to God had been unrewarded and useless, and that his own death was imminent. He even thought death would be "the land of forgetfulness" where all his sorrows and failures could be forgotten.

There is no reason for a Christian ever to feel so despondent. The ungodly man may use the year's end as a time of revelry, hoping to drown the memory of all *his* failures and sins. Cartoonists often depict the old year as a tottering old man, good for nothing and ready to die, while the New Year is like an energetic child, full of hope.

Those who know the Lord must not give way to regretting and forgetting their failures. Inevitably their past blessings will be found to have been greater than their sorrows, when they remember David's testimony. "Bless the Lord, O my soul, and forget not all his benefits . . . who crowneth thee with lovingkindness and tender mercies" (Ps. 103:2–4). As the old hymn would remind us, "Count your many blessings; name them one by one, and it will surprise you what the Lord hath done."

Even in the midst of dreadful devastation and sorrow, if necessary, the believer can say with Jeremiah, "It is of the Lord's mercies that we are not consumed, because his compassions fail not. They are new every morning: great is thy faithfulness" (Lam. 3:22–23).

We can make a wonderful biblical resolution for the New Year: "I will bless the Lord at all times: his praise shall continually be in my mouth" (Ps. 34:1). We must not drift off into the land of forgetfulness, but rather learn daily to dwell in God's Promised Land.

HOW MANY DAYS
DO WE HAVE?

"So teach us to number our days, that we may apply our hearts unto wisdom" (Ps. 90:12).

This admonition is from the great psalm written by Moses as he was about to finish his long life of service to God. Although he had lived 120 years, he wrote that the normal life span would thenceforth be 70 or 80 years. Actually, his early years were spent serving the Egyptians, so his service for God occupied only some 80 years at most, and much of that time he was in the desert away from his people. It was only after he had passed that normal 80-year life span that he actually led his people from Egypt to the Promised Land.

Probably that was in his mind as he stressed the importance of "numbering our days," so that we may determine to use wisely whatever time we have left. He also wrote, in Deuteronomy 32:29: "O that they were wise, that they understood this, that they would consider their latter end!"

Actually, a person with a 70-year life span only has a total of about 18,000 days of potentially useful service for the Lord, assuming his first 20 or so years must be spent in education and training. It may be much less than this, depending on how much of one's mature life is spent in other pursuits than those to which God has called him or her. Each Christian would be well advised to "number the days" he may still have before the Lord comes or death overtakes him. "Boast not thyself of to morrow; for thou knowest not what a day may bring forth" (Prov. 27:1).

Whether this New Year brings chaos, as many have predicted, its days will still afford opportunities to serve the Lord. Therefore, let us resolve to "walk circumspectly, not as fools, but as wise, redeeming the time, because the days are evil" (Eph. 5:15–16).

We should not only count our days, but make our days count, and count for Him!

Creation and the New Year

"In the beginning God created the heaven and the earth" (Gen. 1:1).

It is appropriate for Christians to begin the New Year by referring back to the beginning of the very *first* year. The first verse of God's Word is also its most important verse, since it is the foundation on which everything else is built. Even God's great work of salvation is irrelevant and futile without His prior work of creation, for only the *Creator* of all things could ever become the *Savior* of all things.

If a person really believes Genesis 1:1, he or she should have no difficulty believing anything else in the Bible. The very first object of *saving* faith (Heb. 10:39) is the fact of special creation by the Word of God (Heb. 11:3).

The verse is comprehensive and scientific, viewing space ("the heavens") and matter ("the earth") as functioning in a framework of time ("in the beginning"). This space/matter/time "continuum" (as scientists call it) has not existed eternally, nor is it still being created, both of which heresies are standard beliefs of evolutionary pantheism (including most of the world's religions and philosophies, ancient or modern). It was *created* — and even *completed* — in the past.

This foundation of all foundations is, clearly, the only sure foundation upon which one should build a life, or an organization, or anything. A firm renewal of one's commitment to special creation, as literally recorded by divine revelation in the inerrant Word of God is thus the proper way to begin a New Year, or a new home, or a new career, or a new family, or any phase of a Christian life. This is the time to confess and forsake all doubts, and trust God's word! In the beginning of the *first* year, God created all things. At the beginning of *this* year, we should resolve to believe and obey all things in His Word.

THE BEGINNING
OF THE YEAR

"A land which the LORD thy God careth for: the eyes of the LORD thy God are always upon it, from the beginning of the year even unto the end of the year" (Deut. 11:12).

This phrase, "the beginning of the year," occurs only twice in the Bible — here in Deuteronomy 11:12 and in Ezekiel 40:1. In this passage, the Lord, through Moses, is speaking of the Promised Land which He had prepared for the Children of Israel, "a land of hills and valleys, and drinketh water of the rain of heaven" (Deut. 11:11) promising great blessing on the land and its people if they obeyed God, but judgment if they disobeyed.

Although these promises were made specifically with reference to Israel, the principle surely would apply worldwide, for God "hath made of one blood all nations of men . . . and hath determined the times before appointed, and the bounds of their habitation; That they should seek the Lord" (Acts 17:26–27). It certainly has applied to America, for God has blessed our nation most abundantly, founded as it was in its beginnings on the principles of God's words. Sadly, however, there are now many signs that His blessings are being withdrawn, with judgment imminent, because of the widespread apostasy and moral decay that has overtaken us.

Here, at "the beginning of the year" (even near the beginning of the millennium), we can pray that America will return to the God of our fathers before it is too late and final judgment falls on our once-blessed nation. In the words of our text, "the eyes of the LORD" are on us, "from the beginning of the year even unto the end of the year."

In addition to prayer, we personally can work and give and vote and live in ways that demonstrate our own personal trust in God and His Word, as well as our deep concern for our families, our churches, our nation, and God's eternal plan for His great creation.

THE BEGINNING
OF MONTHS

"This month shall be unto you the beginning of months: it shall be the first month of the year to you" (Exod. 12:2).

When the Children of Israel came out of Egypt, not only was their manner of life changed, but even the way they kept track of time. A new calendar was established by the Lord beginning around the time of the Exodus, so that each New Year would automatically make them remember their new beginning when God led them out of bondage in Egypt.

This beginning of months, the month Abib, corresponding approximately to our modern April, was to be marked especially by observance of the Passover supper on the 14th day of the month. The lamb was to be selected for each family on the 10th day of the month, and presumably the first nine days were days of preparation, self-examination, and anticipation. The week following was to be marked by the use of unleavened bread in each home. The leaven represented the sin which had been purged from the home symbolically by the sacrifice of the lamb and their deliverance by God from bondage in Egypt when He saw the shed blood (note Exod. 12:13).

Although our annual calendar is different from that of Israel at the time of Moses — and, for that matter, from that of modern Jews who have themselves continued to follow a civil calendar beginning in October — the spiritual significance of their religious New Year can well be applied in our own lives today, especially as we begin the New Year. We can remember that "Christ our passover is sacrificed for us" (1 Cor. 5:7), offering special thanks for our great deliverance from sin and death by our "Lamb of God, which taketh away the sin of the world" (John 1:29). Then, like the redeemed Israelites, we should likewise "Purge out therefore the old leaven . . . the leaven of malice and wickedness;" and we should feast instead on "the unleavened bread of sincerity and truth" (1 Cor. 5:7–8). If we would make — and keep — such New Year's resolutions as these, this month would, indeed, become "the beginning of months" to us.

A GREAT NEW YEAR'S RESOLUTION

"For I determined not to know anything among you, save Jesus Christ, and Him crucified" (I Corinthians 2:2).

When Paul first entered the Greek city of Corinth, he had just come from nearby Athens and his encounter with its humanistic philosophers at Mars' Hill (Acts 17:18–18:1). Corinth, like Athens, was saturated with such worldly wisdom and, in addition, as a great seaport and commercial center, was a city of opulent immorality.

The Apostle, however, did not yield to the natural temptation to impress the Corinthians with his own wisdom. Neither did he come to Corinth to harangue them about the city's wickedness. "For Christ sent me," he said, "to preach the gospel." Therefore he could say: "My speech and my preaching was not with enticing words of man's wisdom. . . . That your faith should not stand in the wisdom of men, but in the power of God" (I Cor. 1:17; 2:4–5).

The gospel which Paul preached was based on the assumption of creation by Christ (note Colossians 1:16, 23), and then centered on the substitutionary death, burial, and resurrection of that Creator (I Corinthians 15:3, 4), in anticipation of its glorious consummation at His return (Colossians 1:20). Though Paul did not speak in terms of the evolutionistic wisdom of the Greek philosophers, he did speak the true wisdom, "Which none of the princes of this world knew: for had they known it, they would not have crucified the Lord of glory" (I Cor. 2:8).

Paul's resolution simply to preach Christ—the Lord of all true wisdom and power and glory—and then to tell lost sinners that He had died for them and conquered death for them, is surely a good resolution for every believing Christian to make upon beginning a new year or a new ministry. It is that message—and only that message—that brings salvation and everlasting life.

APPREHENDED
OF CHRIST

"Not as though I had already attained, either were already perfect: but I follow after, if that I may apprehend that for which also I am apprehended of Christ Jesus" (Phil. 3:12).

The Greek verb twice translated "apprehend" in this verse seems to mean something like "fully possess." Paul used the same word when he prayed that the Ephesians would be able to *comprehend* the love of Christ in all its "breadth, and length, and depth, and height," being "filled with all the fulness of God" (Eph. 3:18–19).

If any Christian could ever have claimed to have attained a "perfect" state in his Christian life, it would seem to have been the great apostle Paul. Yet even Paul had to recognize that he still had much to learn about Christ and a long way still to grow in Christ-like character and conduct. Who, therefore, among us today could ever claim to have reached perfection in his or her Christian life? There may be some indeed who would make such claims, but they would inevitably be disputed by those who know them best. "If we say that we have no sin, we deceive ourselves, and the truth is not in us" (1 John 1:8).

Like Paul, each of us should therefore make a firm commitment that "I count not myself to have apprehended: but this one thing I do, forgetting those things which are behind, and reaching forth unto those things which are before, I press toward the mark for the prize of the high calling of God in Christ Jesus" (Phil. 3:13–14).

What better time could there be to make such a resolution than on the first day of a New Year? We have, as believers saved by grace through faith in Christ, indeed been "apprehended" by Him, so we surely ought to "comprehend" Him in all the fullness of His love and in desiring to attain unto His "high calling" for us.

A NEW SONG
FOR A NEW YEAR

"Sing unto him a new song; play skilfully with a loud noise"
(Ps. 33:3).

This is the first of nine references in the Bible to a "new song." Appropriately, the song of Psalm 33 deals with the primeval event of creation, and it is the first psalm that does so (note also Ps. 104, etc.).

The new song has to be sung with instrumental accompaniment. However, the Hebrew word translated "loud noise" is so translated nowhere else; it is translated many different ways, but perhaps the familiar rendering "joyful sound" (Ps. 89:15) is the most appropriate here. In any case, this new song is of great importance and so should be performed well and joyfully, for it deals with the grandest of themes.

First of all is the great assertion that "the word of the LORD" is always right, and the "works" of the Lord are always of truth (Psalm 33:4). His righteousness and goodness are evident everywhere, to those with eyes to see and hearts to believe (verse 5).

Then there is the vital revelation that God's creation of all things was simply by His mighty word, "the breath of his mouth," accomplished instantly, and not dragged out over long ages of evolutionary trial and error. "He spake, and it was done" (verses 6, 9).

Furthermore, it is a comfort to know that God does not change, though new years come and go. "The counsel of the LORD standeth for ever" (verse 11). "Blessed is the nation whose God is the LORD" (verse 12).

There are many other great themes in this new song, and it would indeed be well to read and rehearse them all as each new year begins, committing ourselves once again to the faithful teaching of His inerrant Word, His magnificent creation, and His great salvation.

FAITH FOR
THE FUTURE

"I know both how to be abased, and I know how to abound: every where and in all things I am instructed both to be full and to be hungry, both to abound and to suffer need. I can do all things through Christ which strengtheneth me" (Phil. 4:12–13).

No reader of these lines is likely ever to be called on to endure such suffering as the hardships experienced by the apostle Paul. These were summarized by him as follows: "In labors more abundant, in stripes above measure, in prisons more frequent, in deaths oft. Of the Jews five times received I forty stripes save one. Thrice was I beaten with rods, once was I stoned, thrice I suffered shipwreck, a night and a day I have been in the deep; In journeyings often, in perils of waters, in perils of robbers, in perils by mine own countrymen, in perils by the heathen, in perils in the city, in perils in the wilderness, in perils in the sea, in perils among false brethren; In weariness and painfulness, in watchings often, in hunger and thirst, in fastings often, in cold and nakedness" (2 Cor. 11:23–27).

All of that was still several years before the end of his ministry which finally was terminated by months in a miserable Roman dungeon and then execution by beheading. Yet he could still say, very near the end, "The Lord shall deliver me from every evil work. . . . Grace be with you. Amen" (2 Tim. 4:18–22).

Our own problems, whatever the coming year may bring, will surely be trivial in comparison. The probability, in fact, is that our blessings will be much greater than our burdens. In any case, we can say with Paul, "I can do all things through Christ which strengtheneth me," and he could still count on God's promise: "My grace is sufficient for thee: for my strength is made perfect in weakness" (2 Cor. 12:9).

THE PSALMIST'S RESOLUTIONS

"I have chosen the way of truth: thy judgments have I laid before me" (Ps. 119:30).

As we Christians examine our weaknesses and failures in the past year (perhaps we could just call them sins!) and resolve to do better in the new year, it is helpful to note some of the resolutions made by the writer of the longest chapter in the Bible, Psalm 119. Perhaps those should be ours as well.

For example, we should deliberately choose the way of truth, as he did, resolving to be scrupulously honest in all our words and relationships. "Incline my heart . . . not to covetousness," he also prays (verse 36), for that indeed is a sin which easily besets us, and we should make that our prayer as well.

He resolved also never to be ashamed of the Lord and His Word. "I will speak of thy testimonies also before kings, and will not be ashamed" (verse 46). Then he determined that he must have fellowship with all true believers in the true God who earnestly seek to keep His Word. "I am a companion of all them that fear thee, and of them that keep thy precepts" (verse 63). He will not complain when God is chastising or testing him. "I know, O LORD, that thy judgments are right, and that thou in faithfulness hast afflicted me" (verse 75).

No matter what happens, he will, like Job, trust God. "Thou art my hiding place and my shield: I hope in thy word" (verse 114). He will believe implicitly in all the words of God, fully rejecting any teachings of men that would deny or distort the Scriptures. "Therefore I esteem all thy precepts concerning all things to be right; and I hate every false way" (verse 128). He will thus fully trust the Lord, deliberately choosing to believe His word above all. "Let thine hand help me; for I have chosen thy precepts" (verse 173).

THE
NEW EARTH

"And I saw a new heaven and a new earth: for the first heaven and the first earth were passed away; and there was no more sea" (Rev. 21:1).

As a new year begins, men and women customarily turn over a "new leaf" and make "new resolutions" for improving their behavior. For the Christian, however, the new year — indeed a whole new life — begins when he or she accepts Christ. "Therefore if any man be in Christ, he is a new creature: old things are passed away; behold, all things are become new" (2 Cor. 5:17).

He receives from Christ a "new commandment . . . that ye love one another" (John 13:34). He has come to "Jesus the mediator of the new covenant" (Heb. 12:24), and, in a sense, he lives in a whole new world.

The ultimate New Year is yet to come, however, when Christ returns — perhaps *this* year, perhaps today! He will surely keep His promise, and "we, according to His promise, look for new heavens and a new earth, wherein dwelleth righteousness" (2 Pet. 3:13). Peter *looked for* this world to come, and so do we, but John — translated in time by the Holy Spirit — actually *saw* the new heaven and new earth, and so shall we someday! In fact, as Isaiah prophesied, when God finally does "create new heavens and a new earth . . . the former shall not be remembered, nor come into mind," so glorious will be that new world (Isa. 65:17).

Then we shall have "a new name written" by Christ himself, sing "a new song" with new voices, and live in that "holy city, New Jerusalem" (Rev. 2:17; 5:9; 21:2). We shall have new bodies, new homes, new ministries, new lives, forever. In fact, the Lord Jesus assured John: "Behold, I make all things new. . . . these words are true and faithful" (Rev. 21:5). *All* things will be eternally new in that great new year soon approaching.

ALL THINGS NEW

"And he that sat upon the throne said, Behold, I make all things new. And he said unto me, Write: for these words are true and faithful" (Rev. 21:5).

The coming of a new year is a good time to consider that glorious time to come when Christ will make everything new again. In the present age, all things "shall wax old as doth a garment" (Heb. 1:11) under the bondage of the universal law of decay and death; indeed "the whole creation groaneth and travaileth in pain together until now" (Rom. 8:22).

"Nevertheless we, according to his promise, look for new heavens and a new earth, wherein dwelleth righteousness" (2 Pet. 3:13). There, in the "New Jerusalem," we shall each have "a new name" and sing "a new song" (Rev. 21:2; 2:17; 5:9). We shall have new bodies, "fashioned like unto his glorious body" (Phil. 3:21), and a new dwelling place, prepared by Christ himself among the "many mansions" in His "Father's house" (John 14:2).

All the old and dying things will be completely and forever gone. "There shall be no more death, neither sorrow, nor crying, neither shall there be any more pain: for the former things are passed away" (Rev. 21:4). "And the ransomed of the LORD shall return, and come to Zion with songs and everlasting joy upon their heads: they shall obtain joy and gladness, and sorrow and sighing shall flee away" (Isa. 35:10).

What a "Happy New Year" that will be! In the meantime, we have His "new covenant" and have each been made "a new creature" in Christ (Heb. 12:24; Gal. 6:14). Since all His words "are true and faithful," we know His promises are sure. Therefore, already, "old things are passed away; behold all things are become new" through faith in Christ (2 Cor. 5:17).

Chapter IV

HONORING PARENTS

Two holidays in honor of our parents have become official only in the 20th century, but somewhat similar recognitions actually were customary in ancient Greece. In any case, it surely is fitting to have special days to express love and gratitude for both father and mother. After all, one of God's Ten Commandments says, "Honor thy father and thy mother: that thy days may be long upon the land which the LORD thy God giveth thee" (Exod. 20:12). This was confirmed and even strengthened through the apostle Paul in the New Testament: "Honor thy father and mother; (which is the first commandment with promise); That it may be well with thee, and thou mayest live long on the earth" (Eph. 6:2–3).

In this country, Mother's Day was made an official holiday in 1914 by an act of Congress, designating the second Sunday in May as a day "for public expression of our love and reverence for the mothers." More recently, Father's Day has been somewhat less formally recognized on the third Sunday of June each year. There is also a recently suggested Grandparents Day on the second Sunday in September, but this is not very widely observed as yet.

In any case, it is fairly common, as well as appropriate, to include our grandmothers and grandfathers in the recognition given our parents on *their* designated days. In fact, it is also proper, when so desired, to include *all* our forefathers and foremothers for accolades as the honored founders of the American republic.

THE MOTHER
OF US ALL

"And Adam called his wife's name Eve; because she was the mother of all living" (Gen. 3:20).

Sarah, Abraham's wife, was called the mother of all "the children of promise" (Gal. 4:28), and the wife of Noah was the mother of all post-Flood mankind, but mother Eve, alone, was "the mother of all living." "Adam was first formed, then Eve," Paul said in 1 Timothy 2:13, and so-called "Christian evolutionists" have never yet been able to explain God's unique formation of Eve's body in any kind of an evolutionary context.

Eve, as our first mother, experienced all the great joys and great sorrows that all later mothers would know. She evidently had many "sons and daughters" (Gen. 5:4), and probably lived to see many generations of grandchildren. With Adam, she had even known paradise, but sin had entered their lives when they rebelled against God's Word, and God had to say, "In sorrow thou shalt bring forth children" (Gen. 3:16). The greatest sorrow was no doubt when Cain slew Abel, and as with another mother whose Son's innocent blood was shed many years later, it was like a sword piercing her own soul (Luke 2:35).

Nevertheless, as near as we can tell, after her first great sin, Eve trusted God's Word henceforth, and received His forgiveness and salvation. Later, as the mother of Seth, she taught him and her grandson Enos about the Lord and all His promises. "Then began men to call upon the name of the LORD" (Gen. 4:26).

Most Christian believers are looking forward to seeing their own mothers again someday — restating their love and appreciation for all they did in bearing them, and in caring, teaching, and praying for them. It will be a wonderful experience to meet our first mother, also, as well as Sarah, Hannah, and all the other godly mothers of old.

THE VIRTUOUS WOMAN

"Who can find a virtuous woman? for her price is far above rubies" (Prov. 31:10).

The famous passage on "the virtuous woman" (Prov. 31:10–31) is often used on Mother's Day, so the description of the attributes of such a woman is already well known. It is not so well known that these 22 verses were originally put together in the form of an acrostic, with each verse starting, in turn, with the successive 22 letters of the Hebrew alphabet. It is as though the compiler of Proverbs wanted to conclude the book with a special tribute to his own mother (verse 1), and to imply in so doing that it would exhaust all the resources of human language!

However, the translators have slightly misled the modern generation by using the word "virtuous," which tends to make us think primarily today simply of moral purity. This woman was far more than just that. The Hebrew word, when used as an adjective or adverb describing a woman, was always translated "virtuous" (Ruth 3:11; Prov. 12:4; 31:10) or "virtuously" (Prov. 31:29). When used in reference to men, however (as it is far more frequently), it is always translated by such words as "strong," "valiant," "worthy," etc. Its most common translation is "army." Thus, an ideal woman is a strong, brave, industrious, trustworthy woman, worth an entire army to her husband and her children and her nation. This is woman as God intended woman to be. She is, most especially, a *godly* woman. "Favor is deceitful, and beauty is vain: but a woman that feareth the LORD, she shall be praised" (verse 30).

"Her children arise up, and call her blessed; her husband also, and he praiseth her" (verse 28). This verse is usually acknowledged on Mother's Day, but let us remember that "Honor thy . . . mother" (Exod. 20:12), means every day of the year as well!

THE FAITH
OF OUR MOTHERS

"When I call to remembrance the unfeigned faith that is in thee, which dwelt first in thy grandmother Lois, and thy mother Eunice; and I am persuaded that in thee also" (2 Tim. 1:5).

The "dearly beloved son" (verse 2) of the apostle Paul, was a young disciple whose strong and sincere Christian faith was due, more than anything else, to the lives and teachings of a godly mother and grandmother. As Paul wrote to Timothy, in his last letter, "From a child thou hast known the holy scriptures, which are able to make thee wise unto salvation through faith which is in Christ Jesus" (2 Tim. 3:15).

Timothy's mother was a Christian Jew (Acts 16:1), but his father was a Greek who evidently was not a believer. In the ideal Christian home, the father is to assume spiritual leadership (Eph. 5:22, 25; 6:4), but countless fathers, for some reason, are either unable or unwilling to do this. Many have been the homes where a mother or grandmother, usually by default, has had to assume this all-important responsibility, and the Christian world owes these godly women a great debt of gratitude. The writer himself was raised in such a home, and much of his own concern for the Word of God is due to the concerned dedication of a Christian mother and two Christian grandmothers.

It is significant that the fifth of God's Ten Commandments requires children to honor their parents, and it is the only one of the ten which carries a special promise: "Honor thy father and mother; which is the first commandment with promise; That it may be well with thee, and thou mayest live long on the earth" (Eph. 6:2–3). Every godly parent is worthy of real honor, every day — not just once each year. When a Christian mother, like Timothy's mother, must assume all the responsibility for leading her children in the ways of God, she deserves very special praise.

THE LOVE OF A Christian mother is invaluable in the life of a child. Long before Paul led young Timothy to the full knowledge of Christ, he had "known the holy scriptures, which are able to make thee wise unto salvation through faith which is in Christ Jesus" (2 Tim. 3:15). This was because of the teachings of his mother and grandmother when he was a young child.

FROM
A CHILD

"And that from a child thou hast known the holy scriptures, which are able to make thee wise unto salvation through faith which is in Christ Jesus" (2 Tim. 3:15).

A child who is being taught the Holy Scriptures, such as little Timothy was, has a wonderful advantage from the very beginning. Statistics have shown overwhelmingly that most genuinely Christian adults accepted Christ while still young.

As in Timothy's case, it is usually the mother who has been mainly responsible for teaching the Scriptures to her children. Paul had not even met Timothy until he was already a young man, but then he could "call to remembrance the unfeigned faith that is in thee, which dwelt first in thy grandmother Lois, and thy mother Eunice" (2 Tim. 1:5).

A godly mother and grandmother are of inestimable blessing to their families. Each one "looketh well to the ways of her household," and in due time "Her children arise up, and call her blessed; her husband also, and he praiseth her" (Prov. 31:27–28).

A godly father or grandfather or pastor or Sunday school teacher or some Christian friend may well exert a great influence for good in a child's or young person's life, but a mother who loves the Lord, studies the Scriptures, and teaches them to her children, has a value "far above rubies" (Prov. 31:10) and receives a double reward — first when she sees her son or daughter grow into a spiritually strong and fruitful Christian man or woman — then later, when she will surely hear her own loving Savior say, "Well done, thou good and faithful servant . . . enter thou into the joy of thy lord" (Matt. 25:21).

May today's young mothers seek diligently to follow in the spiritual footsteps of Timothy's Eunice and Lois!

THE PROPHET'S CHAMBER

"And she said unto her husband, Behold now, I perceive that this is an holy man of God, which passeth by us continually. Let us make a little chamber, I pray thee, on the wall; and let us set for him there a bed, and a table, and a stool, and a candlestick: and it shall be, when he cometh to us, that he shall turn in thither" (2 Kings 4:9–10).

This sparsely furnished little room, built by a kindly woman and her elderly husband, was the prototype of all the so-called "prophet's chambers" that have been built for traveling teachers and evangelists ever since.

Little did this simple farm couple anticipate what fruit their kindness would bear one day in this very room. "Be not forgetful to entertain strangers" the Bible says, "for thereby some have entertained angels unawares" (Heb. 13:2). In the first place, to show his appreciation, Elisha prayed that the Lord would give them a son, and God miraculously answered (2 Kings 4:16–17).

Then, tragically, the boy died quite suddenly several years later while Elisha was at Mount Carmel, some 15 miles away. The Shunammite woman laid her son on Elisha's bed in the prophet's chamber, then rode hastily to find Elisha and bring him to the boy. The round trip must have taken her two days or more, and the boy's dead body lay on the prophet's bed in the little room all that time.

Elisha prayed again, and an amazing event took place there (2 Kings 4:33–35). For only the second time in history (1 Kings 17:22), a dead person was restored to life.

The Shunammite mother and her son are never heard from again. For 3,000 years, the testimony of a little chamber and the love and faith of the godly woman who prepared it as a simple service for her Lord and His prophet, and the godly mother who sacrificially loved her son, has been an inspiration and example to multitudes.

THE ELECT
LADY

The elder unto the elect lady and her children, whom I love in the truth; and not I only, but also all they that have known the truth" (2 John 1).

The Greek word for "lady" (*kuria*) is used only two times in the Bible, and both of these occurrences are here in the one-chapter epistle of 2 John. It is also fascinating to note that *kuria* is the feminine form of *kurios*, which is the Greek word for "Lord."

Evidently this "elect lady" was a special woman, very highly esteemed by the apostle John as a capable and conscientious mother to her children.

It is uncertain, however, whether this distinguished lady was a literal mother in the church with literal children or possibly a metaphor for the church itself, with the "children" its individual members. Good reasons can be given for both interpretations, and it may even be that John wrote his letter with this dual meaning in mind under the inspiration of the Holy Spirit.

In either case, it is significant that this mother is called "lady" instead of the much more frequently used "woman" (Greek, *gune*), or even "mother" (Greek *meter*). The Greek *kuria* was evidently used to stress deep respect and honor to such a mother in the church. She clearly was training her children in "the truth," much as Timothy's mother, Eunice, and grandmother, Lois, had brought him up to have "unfeigned faith" in "the holy scriptures, which are able to make thee wise unto salvation through faith which is in Christ Jesus" (2 Tim. 1:5, 3:15).

In addition to faith in God's truth, of course, there should be genuine love. The second use of *kuria* is in verse 5: "And now I beseech thee, lady, not as though I wrote a new commandment unto thee, but that which we had from the beginning, that we love one another" (2 John 5).

THE CLOTHING OF
A GODLY WOMAN

"Strength and honor are her clothing; and she shall rejoice in time to come" (Prov. 31:25).

A lovely little song of the 1930s was called "Try a Little Tenderness." Most readers will not remember it, but all those who have had caring, self-sacrificing mothers can relate to one of its stanzas: "She may be weary: women do get weary, wearing that same shabby dress. And when she's weary, try a little tenderness."

This writer had such a mother, and this familiar chapter on the virtuous woman (Prov. 31:10–31) always reminds him of her. As essentially the main support of three young sons in a depression-era divorced household, she managed to provide food, clothing, and shelter for the family by a succession of low-paying jobs, and with little thought of her own needs.

Many women today, on the other hand, seem concerned mainly with their own personal appearance, spending freely on the latest fashions, and on being well-dressed. A godly woman is one whose apparel is "strength and honor" first of all.

The apostle Paul advised that "women adorn themselves in modest apparel . . . not with braided hair, or gold, or pearls, or costly array; But (which becometh women professing godliness) with good works" (1 Tim. 2:9–10).

Peter said their apparel should "not be that outward adorning of plaiting the hair, and of wearing of gold, or of putting on of apparel," but rather "the ornament of a meek and quiet spirit, which is in the sight of God of great price" (1 Peter 3:3–4).

These Bible verses will remind many of their own godly mothers and also (in the case of this writer, at least) of the mother of their own children. Such mothers will indeed have occasion to "rejoice in time to come."

A WONDERFUL
MOTHER-IN-LAW

"And Ruth said, Entreat me not to leave thee, or to return from following after thee: for whither thou goest, I will go; and where thou lodgest, I will lodge: thy people shall be my people, and thy God my God" (Ruth 1:16).

It is customary to honor our mothers and grandmothers on this special day, and this is surely appropriate, but what about mothers-in-law? Sadly, these good women are too often the object of rude jokes. Perhaps some particular mother-in-law may warrant this kind of treatment, but that would be a rare exception. Most of them (at least in this writer's experience) are sincere, caring women who appreciate and encourage the chosen spouses of their children.

A wonderful example in the Bible is that of Naomi, the honored mother-in-law of Ruth. This is one of the most familiar and best-loved records in the Old Testament.

Ruth was a young widow in the land of Moab, living with Naomi, an older widow originally from Israel. Naomi and her husband and their two sons had migrated to Moab because of a severe famine in their home land. Naomi's husband and two sons had all died there in Moab, leaving Naomi and two daughters-in-law, Orpah and Ruth. When Naomi felt she should return to her home in Bethlehem, Israel, Ruth insisted that she wanted to go with her.

Ruth was thus not only willing to leave her own country, but even to abandon her pagan Moabite religion and to worship Naomi's God — the true God — in order to be with her mother-in-law. What a wonderful godly example Naomi must have been to elicit such love and loyalty from young Ruth!

Then as a testimony of God's amazing grace, Ruth herself was honored by having King David become one of her descendants, through Boaz, her new and honorable second Israelite husband (Ruth 4:21–22). Naomi indeed was a very special mother-in-law.

HONORING
OUR FATHERS

"Honor thy father and thy mother: that thy days may be long upon the land which the LORD thy God giveth thee" (Exod. 20:12).

This familiar command was the fifth in God's list of Ten Commandments, the law of God, and it has never been abrogated. It was quoted by Christ as His own command, when He said: "If thou wilt enter into life, keep the commandments. . . . Honor thy father and thy mother" (Matt. 19:17–19). The apostle Paul also cited it as of special significance: "Honor thy father and mother; (which is the first commandment with promise)" (Eph. 6:2).

This all indicates that God considers the honoring of parents by their children to be of great significance. Since the father has been charged with the primary spiritual responsibility for his family, it is of supreme importance that fathers lead their children properly and the children follow that lead with all due respect and diligence. God blessed Abraham as "the father of us all" (Rom. 4:16) because He could say concerning Abraham: "For I know him, that he will command his children and his household after him, and they shall keep the way of the LORD, to do justice and judgment" (Gen. 18:19).

It is not easy being such a father, but it is vital if our children are to come also to honor their Heavenly Father. "For what son is he whom the father chasteneth not? . . . Furthermore we have had fathers of our flesh which corrected us, and we gave them reverence: shall we not much rather be in subjection unto the Father of spirits, and live?" (Heb. 12:7–9).

"And, ye fathers, provoke not your children to wrath: but bring them up in the nurture and admonition of the Lord" (Eph. 6:4). If we fathers diligently follow God's word in leading our children, then they will honor their fathers, not only while they are children, but all their lives.

The First Commandment with Promise

"Honor thy father and mother; (which is the first commandment with promise); That it may be well with thee, and thou mayest live long on the earth" (Eph. 6:2–3).

The secularists in our society, whose influence is growing and will prove deadly if it continues to grow, have been trying to get God's Ten Commandments (Exod. 20:3–17) purged from public life and recognition, although all sound historians and jurists know that they are the very foundation of our American legal system.

The two "tables" of the Law deal first with our responsibilities under God (the first four commandments) and then to our fellow man (the other six). Of the latter, the first stresses the vital importance of parents in the life of each generation of young people. Not only was this commandment placed ahead of those against murder, adultery, and robbery, but it was the only one specifically promising blessing for obedience, "that thy days may be long upon the land which the LORD thy God giveth thee" (Exod. 20:12).

Today there often seems to be a serious "generation gap" between the interests and standards of parents and their children, even among Christian families, and this is a tragedy. "Children, obey your parents in all things: for this is well pleasing unto the Lord" (Col. 3:20). The Greek word here for "children" can and does apply to children of any age.

Fathers also have a great responsibility. They are commanded to see that their instructions are soundly biblical and spiritually motivated. "Fathers, provoke not your children to anger, lest they be discouraged" (Col. 3:21). "Bring them up in the nurture and admonition of the Lord" (Eph. 6:4). Then it can indeed come to pass that "the glory of children are their fathers" (Prov. 17:6).

FATHER OF ALL
BY CREATION

"Have we not all one Father? hath not one God created us? why do we deal treacherously every man against his brother, by profaning the covenant of our fathers?" (Mal. 2:10).

The message of Malachi, the last of the Old Testament prophets, was primarily directed to the Jews of the restoration, who already were backsliding after being restored from their Babylonian captivity, and God's rebuke of their sinful behavior focused on the key to its correction. They needed to remember, first of all, that they were all brothers, because they all had the same Father. This was not a reference to their becoming spiritual children of God by the new birth, but a reminder of the even more basic fact that they had all been specially created by God in the first place. They should therefore be united in God's great calling of the Jews as God's chosen people, bearing His message to the whole world.

Although Malachi's message was primarily for the Jews, it also has all men in view. "For from the rising of the sun even unto the going down of the same my name shall be great among the Gentiles . . . saith the Lord of hosts" (Mal. 1:11). There was an earlier covenant than the Mosaic and Levitical covenants — one which God made with all men after the great Flood, which has never been withdrawn.

This Noahic covenant, continuing for perpetual generations, does indeed remind us that all men everywhere are brothers, created by the selfsame Creator, and responsible to Him for their behavior toward one another, and for their stewardship of the earth under His ownership. Thus, Malachi's rhetorical questions remind us that the only way to resolve problems among the nations of the world is, first of all, to remind and try to convince them that they all were created by the one true "Lord of hosts," that they must someday answer to Him, and that He still loves them as a father loves his children.

OUR
HEAVENLY FATHER

"Let your light so shine before men, that they may see your good works, and glorify your Father which is in heaven" (Matt. 5:16).

These familiar words were spoken by the Lord Jesus in His so-called "sermon" on the mount — actually a set of instructions primarily addressed to disciples (note Matt. 5:1–2). Jesus often spoke about *your* Father in heaven, when speaking to a number of His disciples together (e.g., Matt. 18:10, and many others, with our text above being the first). He also called Him "*thy* father" when speaking to an individual believer (e.g., Matt. 6:4, 6 — the King James translation follows the Greek original in thus distinguishing between second person singular and plural pronouns).

When talking about His own unique relation to the Heavenly Father, on the other hand, the Lord Jesus spoke directly of *My* Father (e.g., Matt. 7:21; 10:32). Although all born-again believers are "sons of God" (John 1:12), the Lord Jesus Christ is the "only begotten Son" of God (John 3:16), "whose goings forth have been from of old, from everlasting" (Mic. 5:2).

The distinction between *His* relation to the Heavenly Father and *ours* is especially noted in the first words Jesus uttered after His resurrection. Mary Magdalene was the first believer to see Him after He returned from the grave. When she recognized Him and perhaps started to touch Him, He said: "Touch me not; for I am not yet ascended to my Father" and then He said: "I ascend unto my Father, and your Father" (John 20:17). He did not say "ascend to *our* Father." Our own relation to the Father in heaven is beautifully typified by the relation we *should* have to our earthly fathers. Just as a good son desires to honor his human father in word and deed, so Jesus exhorted us to glorify our Heavenly Father by our lives here on earth.

THE GOD OF
OUR FATHERS

"And he said, The God of our fathers hath chosen thee, that thou shouldest know his will, and see that Just One, and shouldest hear the voice of his mouth" (Acts 22:14).

This phrase, "God of our Fathers," and equivalent phrases occur more than 70 times in the Bible. It is important for us to realize that the God whom we worship today is the same God whom our fathers worshiped when they came to this country and also was worshiped by Noah and Abraham and David thousands of years ago. God does not change with the times. "Jesus Christ the same yesterday, and to day, and for ever" (Heb. 13:8).

Ananias of Damascus, in our text verse, informed the newly converted Saul of Tarsus that he had been chosen by that same God of their fathers to make three great changes in his life. He must learn to know God's will for his life; become able to see with spiritual eyesight the righteous judge of all things; and understand God's revelation in the existing Scriptures and (in Paul's special case) to receive God's new revelation regarding Christ and His church.

God today would give each of us a similar three-fold charge in our own lives. We need to be "filled with the knowledge of his will in all wisdom and spiritual understanding" (Col. 1:9). We need also to pray that "the God of our Lord Jesus Christ, the Father of glory, may give unto [us] the spirit of wisdom and revelation in the knowledge of him: The eyes of [our] understanding being enlightened" (Eph. 1:17–18).

Finally, we need to "be mindful of the words which were spoken before by the holy prophets [that is, the Old Testament Scriptures], and of the commandment of us the apostles of the Lord and Savior [that is, the New Testament Scriptures]" (2 Pet. 3:2). Only thus can Christian fathers today truly honor their fathers and their fathers' God.

THE PATRIARCHS

"And he gave him the covenant of circumcision: and so Abraham begat Isaac, and circumcised him the eighth day; and Isaac begat Jacob; and Jacob begat the twelve patriarchs" (Acts 7:8).

The word "patriarch" comes directly from the Greek and means "first father." Thus, the patriarchs begotten by Jacob were the first fathers of the 12 tribes of Israel.

The Genesis patriarchs are types of all fathers. Adam was *the* patriarch of the human family. Through his sin, death came into the world, and death was first mentioned when God warned Adam he would die (Gen. 2:17).

If Adam is the *dying father*, Noah can be called the *righteous father*. The word "just" (or "righteous") is first used where it says "Noah found grace in the eyes of the LORD" (first mention of "grace"), and then "Noah was a just man" (Gen. 6:8, 9).

Abraham is the *believing father*, for "he believed in the LORD; and he counted it to him for righteousness" (Gen. 15:6). This is the first mention of "believe." Abraham is thus a type of all who are justified by faith. The first mention of sowing (symbolic of witnessing) is with Isaac, the *sowing father*. "Isaac sowed in that land, and received in the same year an hundredfold: and the LORD blessed him" (Gen. 26:12; compare Matt. 13:23).

Jacob was named Israel because "as a prince hast thou power with God and with men, and hast prevailed" (Gen. 32:28). A single Hebrew word, only used here, is translated "power as a prince." Jacob, able to prevail in prayer with the angel of the Lord, is the *powerful father*.

These are the honored patriarchs "of whom as concerning the flesh Christ came" (Rom. 9:5). May all who are fathers today, like they, be believing, righteous, sowing fathers, powerful with God and men.

CHRISTIAN FATHERS ARE INSTRUCTED to "provoke not your children to wrath: but bring them up in the nurture and admonition of the Lord" (Eph. 6:4). An essential part of this instruction must be to read and explain the Bible to them, and they are never too young to start. Obviously, this paternal instruction must also be based on paternal example.

THE PEACE OF
THY CHILDREN

"And all thy children shall be taught of the LORD; and great shall be the peace of thy children" (Isa. 54:13).

This prophetic verse has its primary fulfillment still in the future. Nevertheless, it states a basic principle which is always valid, and which is especially relevant on Father's Day. The greatest honor that children can bestow on a father is a solid Christian character of their own, but that must first be his own gift to them. Before sons and daughters can experience real peace of soul, they must first be taught of the Lord themselves, and the Heavenly Father has delegated this responsibility first of all to human fathers.

The classic example is Abraham, "the father of all them that believe" (Rom. 4:11). God's testimony concerning Abraham was this: "For I know him, that he will command his children and his household after him, and they shall keep the way of the LORD, to do justice and judgment" (Gen. 18:19). This is the first reference in Scripture to the training of children and it is significant that it stresses paternal instruction in the things of God. Furthermore, the instruction should be diligent and continual: "When thou sittest in thine house, and when thou walkest by the way, and when thou liest down, and when thou risest up" (Deut. 6:7).

The classic New Testament teaching on child training has the same message: "Ye fathers, provoke not your children to wrath: but bring them up in the nurture and admonition of the Lord" (Eph. 6:4).

Not wrath, but peace, as our text suggests. Great shall be the peace of our children, when they know the Lord and keep His ways. Great, also, is the joy of a godly father when he can see the blessing of the Lord on his children, and then on his grandchildren. "Children's children are the crown of old men; and the glory of children are their fathers" (Prov. 17:6).

CHILDREN OF THE HEAVENLY FATHER

"For this cause I bow my knees unto the Father of our Lord Jesus Christ, Of whom the whole family in heaven and earth is named" (Eph. 3:14–15).

The word "family" in this verse is *patria* in the Greek, and a better translation is "fatherhood" or "lineage" (as in Luke 2:4 — "the house and *lineage* of David"). While it is good to give due recognition to our earthly parents, especially if they have been godly men and women who tried to lead their families in the ways of the Lord, we must never forget that our *first* Father is our Heavenly Father.

The very first mention of both fathers and mothers in the Bible is found in the account of creation itself, and is a command to *leave* father and mother (Gen. 2:24)! It is obvious that each human family can function only while on earth, and even that can only be temporary, since everyone normally will have been a member of at least two family units — that of their parents and that with their children. It becomes more complicated when one has more than one spouse and possibly two or more sets of children.

We all have *one* Father who cares deeply about us! This is even true for those who don't know about Him or even believe He exists. "For in him we live, and move, and have our being. . . . For we are also his offspring" (Acts 17:28). These words were spoken by Paul to pagan idolaters. Every person is, in this sense, a child of God by the very fact of creation, and God loves him (John 3:16) for that reason.

However, we have all become "children of disobedience" by rebelling against our Maker, and thus have become "dead in trespasses and sins" (Eph. 2:1–3). All must now be "born again," receiving Christ — God's *only* begotten Son — as sin-bearing Savior, to become saved children of God through belief on His name (John 1:12). Then, we can truly rejoice in a loving and everlasting Heavenly Father.

THE GLORY
OF CHILDREN

"Children's children are the crown of old men; and the glory of children are their fathers" (Prov. 17:6).

One of the greatest incentives for godly living by fathers and grandfathers is the example set for one's children and grandchildren, that they may indeed "glory" in their parents and desire to follow in their footsteps, especially with reference to their moral and spiritual example.

It is one of the joys of fatherhood not only to have children but, Lord willing, to see one's grandchildren as well. Most honorable men will also work hard to be able to leave an inheritance to their children first of all and, through them, to their grandchildren. "A good man leaveth an inheritance to his children's children" (Prov. 13:22).

Depending on circumstances beyond his control, it may not be possible to leave a significant material estate to his descendants. Therefore, such promises as these must ultimately be understood in the spiritual sense. Even a poor man can leave a goodly inheritance — an inheritance of love and concern and a godly life. The greatest of all the gifts that one should try to pass on to his children, of course, is to lead them, by witness and example, to saving faith in the Lord Jesus Christ, for that heirloom will last forever.

Even men who are childless in the physical sense can have spiritual children as they witness for Christ in word and deed. Paul, for example, could call Timothy "my dearly beloved son" (2 Tim. 1:2), and he could remind the believers at Corinth that "I have begotten you through the gospel" (1 Cor. 4:15).

Then what a joy it is when someone we have led to Christ begins to lead still others to Him! These become our "children's children" in the great spiritual family of God, and such spiritual grandchildren constitute a most beautiful "crown of old men!"

Chapter V

PATRIOTIC
HOLIDAYS

Although there are many designated days each year that might be recognized as "patriotic" remembrances, three of these are of special note and are therefore included in this chapter. These are, in calendrical order: Memorial Day, Independence Day, and Veterans Day.

Memorial Day (formerly called Decoration Day), usually held on May 30, is a day to honor those in the military services who have sacrificed their lives in battle. It originated in the northern states to honor those who died in the Civil War, but now it is generally observed everywhere in the nation, recognizing all who died in later wars as well.

Independence Day (or called generally just the Fourth of July) is a very popular holiday, commemorating the signing of our Declaration of Independence from Great Britain. It marked the official beginning of the American Revolution, which was not actually completed in victory under the leadership of George Washington until 1781. It had been adopted by the representatives of the 13 original states on July 2, but was not publicly announced until July 4, which thereby became the official date of its declaration to the world.

Veterans Day was originally Armistice Day, celebrating the armistice of November 11, 1918, terminating World War I. As other wars came along, especially World War II, the signing of an armistice ending the First World War seemed not so meaningful, so it soon became customary to observe that date as Veterans Day, honoring all those who had served in the armed forces of our country. Although it is not usually taken as a day off from work, like Memorial Day and the Fourth of July, it is often a day of military parades and other patriotic celebrations.

GOD'S
MEMORIAL DAY

"And God said moreover unto Moses, Thus shalt thou say unto the children of Israel, The LORD God of your fathers, the God of Abraham, the God of Isaac, and the God of Jacob, hath sent me unto you: this is my name for ever, and this is my memorial unto all generations" (Exod. 3:15).

It is surely a good thing that Americans have designated an annual Memorial Day in which we call to remembrance the great sacrifices of those before us who fought and suffered (and often died) to form our nation and preserve its freedom. Without them we would not be here today, and we need to remember them.

It is even more important, however, to remember the God of our fathers, our true Author of liberty. He has established His own memorial, wanting us to remember not only our ancient spiritual forefathers, but also His own great name, Jehovah. "The LORD God" in our text verse is *Jehovah Elohim*. The sense of God's announcement to Moses was that "Jehovah" was the name of the God of Abraham, and in fact, the name of the Creator of the world. Jehovah is the redemptive name of God, while Elohim is His name as omnipotent Creator.

We must always remember this, He says. The word "memorial" is used here for the first time in the Bible, and thus is very significant. We should remember Him as Creator every seventh day, when we devote a day to rest and worship (Exod. 20:8, 11). There is also another day to remember the Lord for His work of redemption. When He became man, dying to save us from our sins, He established a memorial supper, saying: "This do in remembrance of me" (Luke 22:19). Thus, when we observe each weekly Lord's Day, and also whenever we partake of the Lord's Supper, we are really observing a special Memorial Day in His honor, remembering His great name "unto all generations."

THE LORD,
OUR MEMORIAL

"Thy name, O LORD, endureth for ever; and thy memorial, O LORD, throughout all generations" (Ps. 135:13).

It is a good thing on Memorial Day to remember and thank God for all those who have given their lives in defense of our nation and its freedoms and great principles.

It is also good to remember the great political statesmen who were the founders of our country and the framers of its wonderful Constitution — men like Washington, Madison, and others who believed in God and the Bible as they labored and planned and prayed.

The same would apply to the great scientists who founded and developed our various sciences and who also believed in God, the Bible, and creation, seeking in their research simply to "think God's thoughts after Him." These included such brilliant, yet devout men as Boyle, Maxwell, Faraday, Pasteur, Fleming, Morse, and many, many others.

It would be even more important to remember the wonderful Christians who have defended and expounded our biblical faith so effectively — Spurgeon, Moody, and all those godly men and women who were instrumental in leading us to saving faith in Christ, especially our parents and other godly family members. Then the "heroes of the faith" of former ages, as listed so powerfully in Hebrews 11, must never be forgotten.

"Wherefore seeing we also are compassed about with so great a cloud of witnesses, let us lay aside . . . the sin which doth so easily beset us, and let us run with patience the race that is set before us, Looking unto Jesus the author and finisher of our faith" (Heb. 12:1–2).

In Him we have a memorial whose name shall endure forever; as our text above says, "thy memorial, O LORD, throughout all generations."

MAKESHIFT WOODEN CROSSES in many places help us remember that many brave fighters have given their lives to gain and keep our freedom. Some of these have actually been planted in the field where they died.

LEST THOU FORGET

"Only take heed to thyself, and keep thy soul diligently, lest thou forget the things which thine eyes have seen, and lest they depart from thy heart all the days of thy life: but teach them thy sons, and thy sons' sons" (Deut. 4:9).

Some of us can remember the words of a melancholy song of the twenties: "You promised that you'd forget me not: but you forgot to remember." Words like these seem to apply increasingly to our observance of Memorial Day, which was originally established in 1868 to honor the Civil War dead, as well as all those others who have given their lives to establish and preserve our "sweet land of liberty." Now it has become just a holiday, a day for leisure and pleasure, rather than for prayer and thankfulness, at least for most Americans.

Like the Israelites of old, who had been urged by Moses not to "forget the things thine eyes have seen . . . but teach them thy sons, and thy sons' sons," but who did indeed soon forget and go the way of the world, the flesh, and the devil, we Americans have largely forgotten these patriots of the past who sacrificed their lives that we might live in freedom. Especially have we — especially our political, educational, and commercial leaders — largely forgotten the God in whom our forefathers believed, and who answered their prayers for our land.

Because Israel forgot, their land eventually was taken over by strangers and her people dispersed all over the world. America is not immune to judgment either, and we need to remember that, "The wicked shall be turned into hell, and all the nations that forget God" (Ps. 9:17).

In the haunting words of Rudyard Kipling, we surely need to pray: "Lord God of hosts, be with us yet; lest we forget, lest we forget."

PILGRIMS ON
THE EARTH

"These all died in faith, not having received the promises, but having seen them afar off, and were persuaded of them, and embraced them, and confessed that they were strangers and pilgrims on the earth. For they that say such things declare plainly that they seek a country" (Heb. 11:13–14).

This is the heart-touching testimony of the great "heroes of faith" of Hebrews 11. The experiences of all these godly men and women of the past are outlined as an example for us as we pass through the years of our own "pilgrimage" on the earth. "Wherefore seeing we also are compassed about with so great a cloud of witnesses, let us . . . run with patience the race that is set before us" (Heb. 12:1).

There is another group who also gave their own lives, and the testimony of our text seems appropriate for them as well. Once a year, on Memorial Day, we remember in a special way those who died in defense of our own country. They had seen its promises and embraced them and were willing to die for them. Many of those were also Christians, and they loved their country, especially because of its unique Christian heritage and its freedom to practice and propagate their faith.

One of these was this writer's younger brother who died in the jungles of Burma as a young pilot flying the famous "Hump" into China during World War II. Before his death, he had given a faithful Christian witness to many of his buddies as he ran his own race with patience. Many readers of these lines no doubt remember their own friends and loved ones who likewise offered up their lives for God and country.

As we remember them, we surely must remember, with even greater love and appreciation, the One who made the greatest sacrifice of all, "looking unto Jesus the author and finisher of our faith; who for the joy that was set before him endured the cross, despising the shame, and is set down at the right hand of the throne of God" (Heb. 12:2).

A CALL TO REMEMBRANCE

"I have considered the days of old, the years of ancient times. I call to remembrance my song in the night: I commune with mine own heart: and my spirit made diligent search" (Ps. 77:5–6).

It is so easy to forget. The burdens and pressures of these present times easily drown out the voices of the past.

God, however, remembers. It is good also for us to consider the olden days, not simply in sad nostalgia, but for our guidance in the present. With reference, particularly to those instances which the Lord selected to be recorded in Scripture, "they are written for our admonition" (1 Cor. 10:11). Not only were they written as warnings, but also for comfort. "For whatsoever things were written aforetime were written for our learning, that we through patience and comfort of the scriptures might have hope" (Rom. 15:4).

To the Christian, an annual Memorial Day should have still an additional special meaning. Not only do we desire to honor those who died for their country (and many of us do, indeed, recall with deep love and respect close friends and family members in this honored company), but also to remember those who lived for the Lord, and whose lives and ministries have helped guide us to the light for our own difficult pathways today. Parents and teachers, authors and preachers, counselors and friends — many of whom have already gone to be with the Lord — deserve to be remembered and honored, for it will make that great future Homecoming Day all the more blessed when we are all together with the Lord when He returns (1 Thess. 4:17).

Most importantly of all, of course, we must remember the Lord, not annually, but always. "I will remember the works of the LORD: surely I will remember thy wonders of old. I will meditate also of all thy work, and talk of thy doings" (Ps. 77:11–12).

A Day to
Remember

"And this day shall be unto you for a memorial; and ye shall keep it a feast to the LORD throughout your generations; ye shall keep it a feast by an ordinance for ever" (Exod. 12:14).

The above command was given to the Children of Israel by God through Moses, as He was preparing to lead them away from slavery in Egypt into the Promised Land to establish their own free nation. On that day, an angel of death would slay every first-born son in Egypt, except that he would "pass over" the homes of the Israelites because of the blood of a slain lamb sprinkled on the lintels and door posts of their houses. That particular date would thereafter be made an annual "memorial day," called Passover, throughout future generations.

Our forefathers, who established our own United States of America, often felt that there was a kind of spiritual analogy between the deliverance of Israel from Egypt and our deliverance from a despotic king in England via our War of Independence. Memorial Day (originally called Decoration Day) was established about the time of the Civil War as a special holiday honoring those who had died in a war fighting to establish or preserve our freedoms.

Just as Israel often forgot to observe their Passover memorial day in later generations, however, so the purpose of our own Memorial Day is often forgotten, with the day being used by most as just another holiday for travel and recreation.

This should indeed be a day to remember and honor all those who have fought and died to maintain our land of the free. If we forget them, we may also soon forget their God and our God, who is the ultimate giver of freedom. We must never forget the sober and fearful warning of Psalm 9:17: "The wicked shall be turned into hell, and all the nations that forget God."

THE PEACE PROCESS

"He maketh wars to cease unto the end of the earth; he breaketh the bow, and cutteth the spear in sunder; he burneth the chariot in the fire" (Ps. 46:9).

For many years now, the Arabs and Israelis have been engaged in a charade called the "peace process," and the other nations have fought two world wars as well as scores of local wars in vain attempts to bring world peace.

In the meantime, multitudes have died in the wars, and we supposedly honor their memory by taking a three-day holiday! One thinks of the scene where the souls under the heavenly altar cry out, saying "How long, O Lord, holy and true, dost thou not judge and avenge our blood on them that dwell on the earth?" (Rev. 6:10). It is not only soldiers who have died. We remember the many who have been slain because of their Christian faith even in modern times (in China, Russia, Sudan, Vietnam, and on and on).

There will indeed come a time when wars will cease! "Nation shall not lift up sword against nation, neither shall they learn war any more" (Isa. 2:4).

The nations need to realize, however, that no permanent world peace will ever be established by the United Nations or any kind of world government. As our text says, it is God who "maketh wars to cease unto the end of the earth."

World peace can only be established and sustained by that One whose name "shall be called . . . The Prince of Peace. Of the increase of His government and peace there shall be no end. . . . The zeal of the LORD of hosts will perform this" (Isa. 9:6–7).

While we await His soon return, we do well to remember and honor those who have died for love of country and, even more, those who have suffered and died for their faith in Christ. "Blessed are the dead which die in the Lord" (Rev. 14:13).

A Good Soldier
of Jesus Christ

"Thou therefore endure hardness, as a good soldier of Jesus Christ. No man that warreth entangleth himself with the affairs of this life; that he may please him who hath chosen him to be a soldier" (2 Tim. 2:3–4).

One of the familiar biblical figures for the Christian life is that we are like soldiers in an army. The weapons and armor are spiritual, but the demands and the discipline are very real. Like military soldiers, we cannot let ourselves get tangled up with the affairs of civilian life. Our obedience must be directed solely to our commanding officer, "the captain of [our] salvation" (Heb. 2:10), the Lord Jesus Christ.

Furthermore, we must be willing to "endure hardness." This is one word in the Greek, used almost exclusively in the New Testament here in this final letter from the apostle Paul before his own martyrdom. He referred to his own situation with the same word, indicating it aided the gospel. "Wherein I *suffer trouble* [same word], as an evil doer, even unto bonds" (2 Tim. 2:9). Paul had been taken a prisoner of war, being sentenced to die as one fighting the state, simply because he was preaching the truth. He even had identified himself as "His prisoner," bound by "my chain . . . ready to be offered" and to give his life for Christ (2 Tim. 1:8, 16–4:6).

What he was willing to do, he urged young Timothy also to be willing to do. "Watch thou in all things, *endure afflictions* [same word], do the work of an evangelist, make full proof of thy ministry" (2 Tim. 4:5). Paul would urge us today, as he urged Timothy, to be willing to endure such things for Christ, who suffered for us and has chosen us to be with Him. The motivation for such willing endurance of hardship is not the prospect of conquest or reward (though these will indeed become realities one day), but simply that we "may please him who hath chosen" us. For those who truly love Him, that is more than enough!

NATIONS
THAT FORGET

"The wicked shall be turned into hell, and all the nations that forget God" (Ps. 9:17).

The prophet Ezekiel once had a remarkable vision of some of the ancient nations that had been cast into hell. All had been founded by men who had once known the true God of creation, but had all forgotten Him as they gradually descended into apostasy. "Son of man, wail for the multitude of Egypt, and cast them down, even her, and the daughters of the famous nations. . . . The strong among the mighty shall speak to him out of the midst of hell with them that help him. . . . Asshur is there and all her company. . . . There is Elam and all her multitude. . . . There is Meshech, Tubal, and all her multitude. . . . There is Edom, her kings, and all her princes. . . . of the north, all of them, and all the Zidonians. . . . even Pharaoh and all his multitude, saith the Lord GOD" (Ezek. 32:18–32).

These nations in hell (i.e., Sheol, the great abyss in the center of the earth) are not nations per se, of course, but the ungodly people, especially the leaders, of those nations. Right after the warning in our text, the Psalmist concludes by saying, "Put them in fear, O LORD: that the nations may know themselves to be but men. Selah" (Ps. 9:20).

Is it possible that such a fate awaits even a nation like America? It is good that many in our nation are taking God more seriously today, but will it last? It is important to remember and honor our founding fathers, and the other heroes of past and present, but infinitely more important not to forget God as so many of our people have done during the past half-century. Not just any "god," of course, but the one true God of creation and salvation, the Lord Jesus Christ. "For all the gods of the nations are idols: but the LORD made the heavens" (Ps. 96:5).

LEST WE
FORGET

"Only take heed to thyself, and keep thy soul diligently, lest thou forget the things which thine eyes have seen, and lest they depart from thy heart all the days of thy life: but teach them thy sons, and thy sons' sons" (Deut. 4:9).

This admonition was given by God through Moses as the Children of Israel were preparing finally to enter God's Promised Land. God had done mighty things for them (delivering them from slavery in Egypt, parting the Red Sea for them, feeding them for 40 years with water from a great rock, and daily bread from heaven) and it was important for them to teach their descendants, "lest thou forget the things which thine eyes have seen."

It was especially vital not to forget the actual words of God. "Ye shall not add unto the word which I command you, neither shall ye diminish ought from it" (Deut. 4:2). The writer of Psalm 119 (the longest chapter in the Bible) stressed no less than seven times how important it was not to forget the words of God.

"I will not forget thy word" (verse 16).

"Yet do I not forget thy statutes" (verse 83).

"I will never forget thy precepts" (verses 93 and 141).

"For I do not forget thy law" (verses 109 and 153).

"For I do not forget thy commandments" (verse 176).

Our nation has seen God do marvelous things. It was founded by a small band of Christians, and in a short span of history has become the greatest nation in the world. Yet we also seem about to forget, as Israel once did.

We would do well to rehearse again and again the poignant words of Kipling, in words written over a hundred years ago:

> Lord God of Hosts, be with us yet
> Lest we forget, lest we forget.

THE BRAVE MEN WHO signed the Declaration of Independence pledged their "lives, property, and sacred honor" to gain liberty for their nation. Many did indeed lose their property in the war, some even lost their lives, but none lost their sacred honor! They are our founding fathers.

LIBERTY THROUGHOUT
THE LAND

"And ye shall hallow the fiftieth year, and proclaim liberty throughout all the land unto all the inhabitants thereof: it shall be a jubilee unto you; and ye shall return every man unto his possession, and ye shall return every man unto his family" (Lev. 25:10).

This verse is especially significant in American history as the verse from which the great exhortation was taken on the first Independence Day: "Proclaim liberty throughout the land to all the inhabitants thereof!" It has ever since been associated with the Liberty Bell and Independence Hall, as Americans each year thank God for "the land of the free."

The verse is also significant as containing the first mention of "liberty" in the Bible. In its biblical context, it established the "jubilee year," when all those Israelites who had sold themselves into bondage were set at liberty. The founding fathers of our nation evidently believed there was a parallel between freedom from bondage to the king of England and freedom from bondage in ancient Israel.

There is even a greater freedom than this. Jesus said, "Whosoever committeth sin is the servant of sin. . . . If the Son therefore shall make you free, ye shall be free indeed" (John 8:34–36). "Know ye not, that to whom ye yield yourselves servants to obey, his servants ye are to whom ye obey; whether of sin unto death, or of obedience unto righteousness? . . . But now being made free from sin, and become servants to God, ye have your fruit unto holiness, and the end everlasting life" (Rom. 6:16–22).

There is always a danger that a free country will someday allow itself to be brought again into bondage, and also a danger that a believer will fall back into sin. To both, God would say, "Stand fast therefore in the liberty wherewith Christ hath made us free, and be not entangled again with the yoke of bondage" (Gal. 5:1).

THE LAW
OF LIBERTY

"So speak ye, and so do, as they that shall be judged by the law of liberty" (James 2:12).

On Independence Day, Americans should give thanks to the Author of liberty that we have been privileged to live in this "sweet land of liberty," where we can worship God freely, in accord with His Word. Liberty is not license, however, and the essence of the American system is liberty *under law*. Fundamentally, that law is "the law of nature and of nature's God," the natural laws of God's world and the revealed laws of God's Word. Within that framework we do have liberty, but not liberty to defy either the physical law of gravity or the spiritual "law of liberty." The latter is formulated in Scripture and has been applied over the centuries, in the English common law and later in our system of constitutional law, both of which are based on Scripture.

Some today, seeking license rather than liberty, might recoil at the very idea of "the *law* of liberty," calling it an "oxymoron," or contradiction in terms. Jesus said that only "the *truth* shall make you free!" (John 8:32). "Sin is the transgression of the law" (1 John 3:4), and "sin, when it is finished, bringeth forth death" (James 1:15), not freedom!

No one can be *saved* by the law, but those who *are* saved — by grace through faith in Christ — will *love* God's law, for it is "holy, and just, and good" (Rom. 7:12). We should say with the Psalmist: "So shall I keep Thy law continually for ever and ever. And I will walk at liberty: for I seek Thy precepts" (Ps. 119:44–45).

There is, indeed, a law of liberty, and whoever will walk in *real* liberty will find it only in God's law of life, through His revealed Word. For "whoso looketh into the perfect law of liberty, and continueth therein, he being not a forgetful hearer, but a doer of the work, this man shall be blessed in his deed" (James 1:25).

TRUE
FREEDOM

"As free, and not using your liberty for a cloak of maliciousness, but as the servants of God" (1 Pet. 2:16).

W e who live in what the songwriter called the "sweet land of liberty" have a great responsibility to preserve that freedom which our forefathers obtained for us at great cost over two centuries ago. At the same time, we must not turn liberty into license. It would surely hurt those brave and godly men if they could see how we now use "freedom of choice" to justify murdering multitudes of innocent children before they are born and how we use "freedom of speech" to warrant fouling the eyes and ears of our children with widespread pornography and to promote all kinds of immoral behavior in our society in general. No nation can remain free very long after such practices become widely accepted by its citizens. We need to pray for revival!

The same warning applies to the abuse of our spiritual freedom in Christ. As the apostle Paul said and repeated, "All things are lawful unto me, but all things are not expedient" (1 Cor. 6:12; also 1 Cor. 10:23, where he added that "all things are lawful for me, but all things edify not").

As Peter says in our text, even though we are "free" and have real "liberty," we are nevertheless "servants of God," where the Greek word *doulos* actually connotes "bond servants," or even "slaves." Our liberty in Christ is not freedom to sin whenever we so choose, but rather freedom from our former bondage to sin. "Being then made free from sin, ye became the servants of righteousness" (Rom. 6:18).

Although our nation is rapidly becoming anti-Christian in belief and practice, we Christians can still best serve our nation and our Savior by practicing and proclaiming Christ's wonderful saving gospel of free salvation from sin and regeneration unto righteousness.

GLORIOUS
LIBERTY

"Because the [creation] itself also shall be delivered from the bondage of corruption into the glorious liberty of the children of God" (Rom. 8:21).

This is the first of 11 occurrences of the noun "liberty" (Greek, *eleu-theria*) in the New Testament. The Christian patriot Patrick Henry became famous for his "liberty or death" speech that helped spur the American people on to liberty from their British bondage. Three millennia earlier, the Children of Israel had been delivered into liberty from bondage in Egypt. The greatest deliverance of all will be when God's mighty universe, now groaning under its great curse of decay and death because of sin (here called "the bondage of corruption"), will be delivered into the glorious liberty already shared by the redeemed children of God.

When Adam's sin brought death into the world (Rom. 5:12), God had to curse the very dust of the ground for man's sake (Gen. 3:17). That is, the basic elements of the physical universe out of which all material substances had been formed have been placed in bondage to a law of decay, with every substance tending toward disintegration and death. In science, this principle is called the law of increasing entropy (or disorder) and is acknowledged as one of its most basic and certain laws.

The Creator who imposed the Curse has also paid the price to deliver His creation, becoming man himself, then dying for man's sin, and defeating death by His resurrection.

One day soon the creation will experience its own glorious freedom when Jesus comes again. As Moses once led Israel out of bondage, and as Washington led America to its freedom, so Christ will deliver His redeemed creation into glorious liberty, forever.

GOD AND
THE GOVERNMENT

"Let every soul be subject unto the higher powers. For there is no power but of God: the powers that be are ordained of God" (Rom. 13:1).

Many difficult questions arise regarding a Christian and his government, but certain principles are very clear. First of all, government is a gift of God, and any form of government is better than anarchism, where "every man did that which was right in his own eyes" (Judg. 21:25). As Paul was writing the words of our text, the monstrous Emperor Nero, who would eventually have Paul executed, was at the height of his power, yet Paul said that whosoever "resisteth the power, resisteth the ordinance of God" (Rom. 13:2).

With this in mind, there are two clear Christian duties: Peter, who later was also executed by Nero wrote, "Submit yourselves to every ordinance of man for the Lord's sake . . . that with well doing ye may put to silence the ignorance of foolish men" (1 Pet. 2:13–15). Again from Paul: "I exhort therefore, that, first of all, supplications, prayers, intercessions, and giving of thanks, be made for all men; For kings, and for all that are in authority; that we may lead a quiet and peaceable life in all godliness and honesty" (1 Tim. 2:1–2).

A Christian can accomplish far more to influence his government and fellow citizens for good by prayer and law-abiding behavior than by complaining, criticizing, and covert disobedience. On the other hand, he is also subject to God's higher law, and he must always remember that "our conversation [or 'citizenship'] is in heaven" (Phil. 3:20), and "we ought to obey God rather than men" (Acts 5:29) whenever there is a conflict between the ordinances of men and the laws of God. To understand and apply these principles in particular situations may be difficult, and may require much further study and prayer, but these are always the basic premises with which to begin.

STAND FAST
IN LIBERTY

"Stand fast therefore in the liberty wherewith Christ hath made us free, and be not entangled again with the yoke of bondage" (Gal. 5:1).

This exhortation from the apostle Paul stresses our deliverance in Christ from legalistic bondage to dead works of religious ritualism. There once had been a divine purpose for all the dietary rules, animal sacrifices, and miscellaneous regulations under the Mosaic laws, but the Jews had lost sight of the spiritual meaning and value of these laws. Their leaders had even expanded them into a great host of special applications which had become a heavy burden to the people, with little spiritual benefit.

"Christ hath redeemed us from the curse of the law" (Gal. 3:13), having "put away sin by the sacrifice of himself" (Heb. 9:26), not that we may have license to live as selfishly and sinfully as we please, but that we might be free to "walk in the Spirit" and "live unto God" (Gal. 5:16; 2:19). This "liberty wherewith Christ hath made us free" is a priceless gift from God, to be defended — not compromised or abused.

Our Christian forefathers originally settled this country and later established our nation primarily to be able to exercise this liberty of serving God according to His Word. Now, just as the Galatians had been in grave danger of losing their freedom in Christ to the Judaizers, so we today are in even greater danger of losing our religious liberties to the secularizers. Our humanist-dominated educational and judicial systems have been able to establish evolutionary humanism as our unofficial state religion, with many legalistic encumbrances to our exercise of true freedom in Christ. How urgently we need today, to "stand fast therefore in the liberty wherewith Christ hath made us free."

TRUE
EQUALITY

"There is neither Jew nor Greek, there is neither bond nor free, there is neither male nor female: for ye are all one in Christ Jesus" (Gal. 3:28).

O ne of the wonderful aspects of America's great Declaration of Independence is its repeated recognition of God as our Creator, beginning with its thrilling assertion that "all men are created equal" and that this fact is "self-evident."

However, it is not self-evident that men are all *born* equal. Even in colonial America, there were those who were bondmen (that is, slaves), and these were not equal politically with their owners. Furthermore, some men were wealthy landowners, some were poor clerks. Women were hardly equal to men in terms of suffrage or wages or various other ways.

As a matter of fact, nowhere in the world has there ever been a society in which all people were true equals in physical beauty, in mental or physical strength, or in many other ways. In truth, such a society would hardly even be desirable if it could ever be produced.

How is it, then, that we are created equal? The only possible answer is that we are equal in God's sight. He is, indeed, the One who has created us and we are all equally responsible to Him.

Yet, "all have sinned," and "there is none righteous, no, not one" (Rom. 5:12; 3:10). Consequently, all people were lost sinners, unfit to enter God's perfect kingdom, but "while we were yet sinners, Christ died for us" (Rom. 5:8), and He is "the propitiation . . . for the sins of the whole world" (1 John 2:2).

When we believe on Christ as our Savior, we each are created equal in Him "after the image of him that created him" (Col. 3:10) — whether Jew or Gentile, slave or free, man or woman — "For ye are all the children of God by faith in Christ Jesus" (Gal. 3:26).

SLAVES OR FREEMEN

"For he that is called in the Lord, being a servant, is the Lord's freeman: likewise also he that is called, being free, is Christ's servant" (1 Cor. 7:22).

Most of us today, rejoicing in our freedoms (of religion, of press, of speech, etc.), tend to forget that these had been purchased for us at great cost. Many of the first Christians, in fact, were actually slaves in the great Roman Empire. The word "servant," as used in the above text, is translated from the Greek *doulos*, the proper meaning of which is "bond-servant," or "slave."

The early Israelites also were slaves for hundreds of years before God empowered Moses to lead them out of Egypt. Later, many were again carried into captivity by the armies of Assyria and Babylon and eventually Rome, continuing to suffer virtual enslavement for many years.

The American colonists were never real slaves, of course, but they often considered themselves as essentially in bondage to the king of England, and their writers frequently compared the American Revolution to the Israelites gaining their freedom from Egypt. An even more apt comparison, however, would have been the setting of the slaves free in the Civil War.

The most appropriate analogy of all, however, applies when a man or woman, having been under control by lifelong sin, is finally set free in Christ, who came to "deliver them who through fear of death were all their lifetime subject to bondage" (Heb. 2:15).

Yet those early believers were never encouraged by Paul to fight for their physical freedom (which would come in good time) but rather to serve their masters "With good will doing service, as to the Lord, and not to men" (Eph. 6:7). He would tell us today not to boast in our own freedom, but to be thankful and to consider ourselves as bondservants to our own Master, the Lord Jesus Christ.

UNITED
WE STAND

"Only let your conversation be as it becometh the gospel of Christ: that whether I come and see you, or else be absent, I may hear of your affairs, that ye stand fast in one spirit, with one mind striving together for the faith of the gospel" (Phil. 1:27).

Paul, writing to the church at Philippi, felt it desirable to urge them to stand unitedly, with "one spirit" and "one mind," "striving together." The latter phrase is one word in the original (*sunathleo*). In this word, the prefix *sun* meant "in union with," while *athleo* referred to competing in the Olympic games. It is the source of our English word "athletics." The combined word, *sunathleo,* translated in our text as "striving together," in effect means "competing unitedly in a bodily contest." Thus, body, mind (or "soul"), and spirit are to be united in a "steadfast stand" as Christians preach the gospel.

It is interesting that the unofficial motto for our nation's current "war on terror" has come to have a very similar connotation ("united we stand") as we fight the ones our president identified as "evildoers."

Our nation today celebrates the hard-won freedom won for us by our forefathers over two-and-a-quarter centuries ago, when 13 colonies strove together to form the "*United* States of America." It is vital that we continue to *stand fast* and *strive together* in this potentially most dangerous of all our nation's wars.

It is most important of all that every Bible-believing Christian continues to "Stand fast therefore in the liberty wherewith Christ hath made us free" (Gal. 5:1) from the bondage and penalty of sin, through faith in His Word.

Finally, we must by all means, in the critical days ahead, continue faithfully "with one mind striving together for the faith of the gospel."

A GODLY HERITAGE

"Blessed is the nation whose God is the LORD; and the people whom he hath chosen for his own inheritance" (Ps. 33:12).

The primary thought of the Psalmist as he wrote these words, no doubt, was in reference to Israel, which did, indeed, have a godly heritage (same word in the Hebrew as "inheritance"). Nevertheless, the promise is broad enough to apply to any nation whose God is the God of Israel, and our own nation has surely experienced great blessing in accordance with this promise. Founded by men and women who settled this country in order to be free to worship the true God of creation and salvation in accordance with the teachings of Holy Scripture, this "one nation under God" has, for over two centuries now, served as the world's chief bastion of religious freedom, as well as Christian missions and evangelism, and God has blessed us abundantly because of it.

It is significant that this promise follows one of the strongest statements of absolute creation to be found in the Bible. "By the word of the LORD were the heavens made; and all the host of them by the breath of his mouth. . . . For he spake, and it was done; he commanded, and it stood fast" (Ps. 33:6–9).

It is no coincidence that America's long-standing recognition of the God of the Bible was founded on the belief of its people in the literal creation record of Genesis. Evolutionary speculations were permeating Europe at that time, but they did not begin to influence American thought until much later.

Just as God will bless any nation whose God is the true God of creation — the God of ancient Israel and the Father of our Lord and Savior Jesus Christ — so He will curse any nation that turns away from Him. "The wicked shall be turned into hell, and all the nations that forget God" (Ps. 9:17).

America, with its great Christian heritage of the past, has been signally blessed by "the God of our fathers." Its rapidly growing apostasy from the true God and His Word is now placing it in deadly peril of God's judgment. Pray, on this Independence Day, that God will forgive our wicked, forgetting nation, and bring us back to the faith of our fathers.

THE STAR-SPANGLED BANNER

"In God have I put my trust: I will not be afraid what man can do unto me" (Ps. 56:11).

The familiar motto on our coins, "In God We Trust," once was the motto of our nation. It is even included in the last verse of our national anthem which seeks to honor our national flag, "The Star-Spangled Banner."

This anthem is sung so often at recreational occasions that it now almost seems trite to many. The venerable banner itself is often dishonored, even burned or trampled on by anti-patriots. Only the first verse of "The Star-Spangled Banner" is used these days, for reasons that become obvious when the last verse is read. Here is that last verse, for those who have never heard it.

> O thus be it ever when free men shall stand
> Between their loved homes and the war's desolations
> Blest with vict'ry and peace, may the heav'n-rescued land
> Praise the Pow'r that hath made and preserved us a nation!
> Then conquer we must, when our cause it is just
> And this be our motto: "In God is our trust!"
> And the Star-Spangled Banner in triumph shall wave
> O'er the land of the free and the home of the brave.

The intellectual elite of our nation no longer believe that a divine Power made our nation or that He in heaven rescued our land here on earth. Most of our people give nominal agreement to the motto on our coins, though they pay little heed to God except in emergencies.

Nevertheless, we do have a godly heritage and there is still a significant minority whose trust in God is real and active. We still shed tears of thankfulness on the Fourth of July and on Flag Day and whenever we see the stars and stripes waving over our sweet land of liberty. We still trust in God and pray for our country, grateful for the privilege of being part of a people so signally blessed by God.

The Peace
from God

"The Lord lift up His countenance upon thee, and give thee peace"
(Num. 6:26).

The beautiful benediction of Numbers 24–26 is climaxed by this prayer for God-given peace. The word for "give" is a very strong word, implying a gift which is permanent and secure. The blessing in effect says: "The Lord *establish* peace for you!"

Men have longed for peace all through history, but always there are those who want war. "I am for peace," the Psalmist said; "but when I speak, they are for war" (Ps. 120:7). Even today, in our "enlightened" age of science and education, there are perhaps 40 local wars raging in the world, and seemingly nothing can be done to stop them.

Those in the "over 65" generation remember how our modern Veterans' Day was once called Armistice Day, established to commemorate the ending of the World War, the "war to end all wars," as we were assured. When World War II came along, then the Korean War and the Vietnam War, as well as various little wars (Grenada, Panama, Iraq, etc., only to mention those directly involving our own country), the term "Armistice Day" soon became obsolete.

It is good and right to remember and honor our military veterans, of course, especially those who gave their lives in such wars, but the world seems further away from true world peace than ever. It will always be so, until the Lord himself lifts up His countenance on His creation and *establishes* peace. Then — but not until then — "of the increase of his government and peace there shall be no end. . . . The zeal of the Lord of hosts will perform this" (Isa. 9:7), when Christ returns. Nevertheless, the believer can, right now, know true and lasting peace of soul, for the Lord Jesus will "keep him in perfect peace, whose mind is stayed on [Him]: because he trusteth in [Him]" (Isa. 26:3).

THE ARMISTICE OF November 11, 1918, celebrated — as wistfully hoped at the time — the end of all war, and it was marked by parades and celebrations in many nations. The prophet Daniel had noted that "unto the end wars and desolations are determined" (Dan. 9:26, literal rendering), and soon the name of the annual Armistice Day was changed simply to Veterans Day. There have been many wars since the so-called "Great War" ended.

To End
All Wars

"And he shall judge among the nations, and shall rebuke many people: and they shall beat their swords into plowshares, and their spears into pruning hooks: nation shall not lift up sword against nation, neither shall they learn war any more" (Isa. 2:4).

It has been over 90 years since the "War to End All Wars" ended in victory for those who had "fought to make the world safe for democracy." A celebration of thanksgiving followed, and a holiday was established to commemorate that great Armistice Day (now Veteran's Day).

However, an even greater war soon followed, only to be repeated by innumerable local wars and revolutions. Instead of a world of liberty and democracy, many of the world's nations are now under the brutal heel of totalitarian dictatorships. With the threat of potential nuclear obliteration hanging over the world, the prophecy of Christ is being literally fulfilled: "Men's hearts failing them for fear, and for looking after those things which are coming on the earth" (Luke 21:26).

In the 25 centuries since our text was first uttered, there has been a war going on somewhere in the world at least 11 out of every 12 years, and it certainly seems unlikely that such a promise will ever be fulfilled.

Yet it is God who has promised, and only He can accomplish it. "*He shall judge among the nations, and shall rebuke many people*" (our text for today). "Of the increase of his government and peace there shall be no end. . . . The zeal of the LORD of hosts will perform this" (Isa. 9:7). When the Lord Jesus Christ comes again, "He shall speak peace unto the [nations]: and his dominion shall be from sea even to sea, and from the river even to the ends of the earth" (Zech. 9:10). Finally, world peace will come, and Christ "shall reign forever and ever" (Rev. 11:15).

PEACEMAKERS

"Blessed are the peacemakers: for they shall be called the children of God" (Matt. 5:9).

In this seventh (out of nine) of the Beatitudes with which Christ began His Sermon on the Mount occurs the first mention in the New Testament of the important word "peace."

How can one be a peacemaker? Note that Christ did *not* say: "Blessed are the pacifists." There are many today who talk about peace, but how does one *make* peace?

The answer lies in the example of Christ, himself. He is the Prince of Peace (Isa. 9:6), and He "made peace through the blood of his cross, by him to reconcile all things unto himself" (Col. 1:20).

The real problem is that there can be no lasting peace between man and man, as long as there is enmity between man and God. "Therefore being justified by faith, we have peace with God through our Lord Jesus Christ" (Rom. 5:1). "And all things are of God, who hath reconciled us to himself by Jesus Christ" (2 Cor. 5:18).

With that problem settled, we are then in a position to become true peacemakers, for we also can lead others to God through Jesus Christ. He "hath given to us the ministry of reconciliation; To wit, that God was in Christ, reconciling the world unto himself, not imputing their trespasses unto them; and hath committed unto us the word of reconciliation. Now then we . . . pray you in Christ's stead, be ye reconciled to God" (2 Cor. 5:18–20).

As ambassadors for Christ, we are true ambassadors for peace. The best possible contribution we can make toward world peace, racial peace, industrial peace, family peace, or personal peace, is to help people become reconciled to God through faith in the peacemaking work of Christ on the cross. "These things have I spoken unto you," says the Lord Jesus, "that in me ye might have peace" (John 16:33).

THE PEACE OF THE
GOD OF PEACE

"And the peace of God, which passeth all understanding, shall keep your hearts and minds through Christ Jesus" (Phil. 4:7).

For generations, most of the world's people have longed for peace, but the world continues to be at war. Evolutionists attribute this to ages of violent evolutionary struggle; the Bible attributes it to sin!

It is wonderfully possible to have real personal peace even in a world at war. This is what the Bible calls "the peace of God," and it surpasses all human understanding, because it is provided by the God of peace, for the writer continues, "The God of peace shall be with you" (verse 9).

The God of peace! There are some wonderful promises associated with this beautiful name of our Lord. For example: "The God of peace shall bruise Satan under your feet shortly" (Rom. 16:20). Also: "The very God of peace sanctify you wholly" (1 Thess. 5:23).

The provision of God's perfect peace (Isa. 26:3) is specifically invoked in 2 Thessalonians 3:16: "Now the Lord of peace himself give you peace always by all means." Perhaps the greatest promise of all is implied in the concluding prayer of the Book of Hebrews: "Now the God of peace, that brought again from the dead our Lord Jesus, that great shepherd of the sheep, through the blood of the everlasting covenant, Make you perfect in every good work to do his will, working in you that which is wellpleasing in his sight through Jesus Christ" (Heb. 13:20–21).

There is only one other reference to *the peace of God:* "And let the peace of God rule in your hearts, to the which also ye are called in one body; and be ye thankful" (Col. 3:15). The peace of God, from the God of peace, can rule in our hearts if we *let* it rule in our hearts. Then, as promised in our text, it will also *keep* our hearts!

WORDS OF
PEACE AND TRUTH

"And he sent the letters unto all the Jews, to the hundred twenty and seven provinces of the kingdom of Ahasuerus, with words of peace and truth" (Esther 9:30).

The Book of Esther is unique in that it contains no explicit mention of God. Yet the hand of God is more evident in this book than in almost any other. It was after their remarkable deliverance from the genocide that had been contrived for them by Haman that Mordecai wrote his "words of peace and truth" to all the Jews, establishing an annual holiday to commemorate the providential winning of peace with their enemies, with the triumph of truth over evil and deception.

This incisive though unusual combination of words ("peace and truth") was also used by Hezekiah when the Lord promised safety for his kingdom as long as he lived. "Is it not good, if peace and truth be in my days?" (2 Kings 20:19). Similarly, God promised His people delivery from their Babylonian captors: "I will cure them, and will reveal unto them the abundance of peace and truth" (Jer. 33:6). Finally, through Zechariah, God promised His people a future lasting peace which they were to commemorate four times a year with "joy and gladness, and cheerful feasts; therefore love the truth and peace" (Zech. 8:19).

Men have longed for peace all through the centuries, but it continues to elude them. After the so-called "war to end all wars," an annual remembrance day called Armistice Day was established to celebrate the lasting peace which that war supposedly secured. Now, of course, it is called Veterans Day — still a day for honor, but hardly one of light and gladness. Peace can only endure in truth.

Although God was never named in the Book of Esther, He was there! Mordecai's "words of peace and truth" implicitly spoke of the Lord Jesus Christ. There will only be real peace when men accept the real truth.

He that
Beareth the Sword

"For he is the minister of God to thee for good. But if thou do that which is evil, be afraid; for he beareth not the sword in vain: for he is the minister of God, a revenger to execute wrath upon him that doeth evil" (Rom. 13:4).

E ver since the great Flood, God has assigned temporal human government to man himself, whether that government has been in the form of a monarchy, democracy, or whatever. This responsibility has even included the authority of capital punishment for certain offenses. Sometimes God even uses one nation to bear the sword against another nation that has incurred His wrath.

It is noteworthy that Paul himself, who wrote the words of our text, was eventually executed by the Roman government headed by a wicked emperor, yet he never resisted. He knew that God would eventually deal with all rulers who misused their authority.

The Lord Jesus himself was put to death by a human government, but neither did He resist (He had established governments in the first place). In time, the Jewish government would be overthrown by the Roman armies, and eventually the Roman empire would be defeated by the armies of those they considered barbarians, and so on.

The individual soldiers in these armies, as well as those who executed Paul and crucified Christ were actually "bearing the sword" of their governments. One soldier at the cross even came to recognize that "this man was the Son of God" (Mark 15:39).

All such soldiers deserve respect, as instruments of God, especially those who personally know the Lord and are "with good will doing service, as to the Lord, and not to men" (Eph. 6:7). These are the true servicemen whom we seek to remember and honor on Veterans Day.

No Discharge
in that War

*"There is no man that hath power over the spirit to retain the spirit;
neither hath he power in the day of death: and there is no discharge
in that war; neither shall wickedness deliver those that are given to it"*
(Eccles. 8:8).

Many readers will still remember the end of World War II, and the
great celebrations that attended the release and homecoming of
the servicemen who had fought in the war. Many more recall the similar
enthusiasm that followed the end of the recent Gulf War, and a few can
even remember when World War I ended with the signing of an armistice
on November 11, 1918, a date still commemorated each year and now
called Veterans Day.

There is a lifelong war going on in the heart and mind of every person
now living, and there is no discharge (or release) in that war, until death
itself. Since the Hebrew word for "spirit" is the same as for "wind," a number of modern translations use "wind" instead of "spirit" in the text verse
above.

However, the whole context seems clearly to refer to our life as an
ongoing battle against death, a battle as it were fought by God in Christ
as against the world, the flesh, and the devil over the destiny of our eternal
spirit. The lying wisdom of this world is "earthly, sensual, devilish" (James
3:15), but "this is the victory that overcometh the world, even our faith"
(1 John 5:4).

We can overcome because Christ is "the captain of (our) salvation"
and "the author and finisher of our faith" (Heb. 2:10; 12:2). When we
trust and follow Him, we are assured of ultimate triumph and release
from the great war. Through His own death and resurrection, He will
"destroy him that had the power of death, that is, the devil; And deliver
them who through fear of death were all their lifetime subject to bondage"
(Heb. 2:14–15).

The
Good Fight

"I have fought a good fight, I have finished my course, I have kept the faith" (2 Tim. 4:7).

The beautiful National World War II Memorial in the nation's capital was dedicated on a recent Memorial Day, honoring the more than 400,000 who gave their lives in that conflict (including the writer's younger brother). This particular holiday today, of course, originally known as Armistice Day, had been established many years before to commemorate the end of World War I, and to honor the veterans of *that* war.

There have been many other wars in our nation's history, and many who have served and many who have died. They all "have fought a good fight" and "kept the faith" of our nation's commitment to establish "liberty and justice for all" and to maintain this ideal in every generation. They fully merit our honor and heartfelt gratitude.

There is another good fight going on, of course, every day in the life of each believing Christian. The apostle Paul never served as a soldier in any human army, but he was often called on to "endure hardness, as a good soldier of Jesus Christ" (2 Tim. 2:3). As a matter of fact, each of us must remember that "unto you it is given in the behalf of Christ, not only to believe on him, but also to suffer for his sake" (Phil. 1:29).

That suffering may be actual persecution, or even injury or death on a battlefield, but it could also be poverty or sickness or some other "messenger of Satan" (2 Cor. 12:7) sent to test us and alienate us from the Lord. Then we can hear the Lord say, as with Paul, "My grace is sufficient for thee: for my strength is made perfect in weakness" (2 Cor. 12:9).

Whatever comes, may God help us to be able to say in that day: "I have fought a good fight, I have finished my course, I have kept the faith."

HE SHALL
SPEAK PEACE

"And I will cut off the chariot from Ephraim, and the horse from Jerusalem, and the battle bow shall be cut off: and he shall speak peace unto the heathen: and his dominion shall be from sea even to sea, and from the river even to the ends of the earth" (Zech. 9:10).

This wonderful prophecy follows immediately after the verse predicting the coming of the Messiah into Jerusalem riding upon a lowly donkey's colt (Zech. 9:9). That prediction was fulfilled by Jesus as He came into Jerusalem on that last Sunday before His death and resurrection (Matt. 21:4–5), but the prophecy in our text was certainly not fulfilled at that time. There have been wars somewhere in the world practically every year since Jesus came, and there are probably 40 or more local wars going on right now. Nevertheless, the day *will come* when He shall indeed speak peace to all the nations.

There was a time just over 85 years ago when the nations had fought a great war that was supposed to end all wars. They celebrated the armistice that ended that war on November 11, 1918, and established an annual holiday called Armistice Day, but many other wars followed that war, so the name was changed to honor the veterans that had fought in any of those later wars as well. However, there is still no real peace in the world.

The fact is that there can be no lasting peace between men and other men until there is peace between men and God. Only the Lord Jesus Christ can make such a peace, for He alone is the "Prince of Peace" (Isa. 9:6). Indeed, He has already paid the price to make such true and eternal peace, for He "made peace through the blood of his cross, by him to reconcile all things unto himself" (Col. 1:20).

In that great coming day when He returns to earth to establish His kingdom, "He maketh wars to cease unto the end of the earth" (Ps. 46:9), "and the LORD alone shall be exalted in that day" (Isa. 2:17).

THE
LAST WAR

"And I saw the beast, and the kings of the earth, and their armies, gathered together to make war against him that sat on the horse, and against his army" (Rev. 19:19).

The end of World War I, the "war to end all wars," as it was once called optimistically and utterly unrealistically, came finally on November 11, 1918, called Armistice Day at the time, and Veterans Day in the years since World War II. We consider our nation a peace-loving nation, yet we have been involved in the War of Independence, the War of 1812, the Mexican War, the American Civil War, the Spanish-American War, World Wars I and II, the Korean War, the Vietnam War, the Gulf War, and currently the strange War against Terror, not to mention a number of local skirmishes (Tripoli, various Indian "wars," Bosnia, etc.) and the Cold War.

It is probably true that there has been at least one local war going on somewhere in the world every year since history began, but one day a war to end all wars will really take place, the great War of Armageddon. This is the war mentioned in our text which also contains the next-to-last mention of war in the Bible. At that time, drawing nearer day by day, Satan will muster all the armies of the nations for one final great assault against Christ and the armies of heaven.

The battle will not last long. All the devil's hosts will be instantly slain by the verbal sword of the man on the white horse, and Satan thrown into the abyss of hades.

Yet there is still one more "battle" (same Greek word as "war") when Satan is released for a time and allowed to "deceive the nations" once more. He will "gather them together to battle" against God one final time (Rev. 20:8). The fire of heaven will destroy them, and the nations shall never "learn war any more" (Mic. 4:3).

Chapter VI

HARVEST HOLIDAYS

There are two main holidays during the fall. One is just at the beginning of the harvest season and is called Labor Day, the other right at the end, called Thanksgiving.

Labor Day is generally observed in the United States and Canada on the first Monday in September. The various labor organizations involved in lobbying for its recognition as an official national holiday succeeded in 1894 when a bill establishing it was passed by Congress. Before that, a similar holiday had sporadically been observed by those involved in the socialist movement in many European countries on May 1. Although the emphasis in this country has traditionally been to note the importance of all the laborers in industry (as well as on the farms) to our national life, it is now observed as a holiday by practically everyone.

Thanksgiving Day is commonly observed on the last Thursday in November as a time for giving thanks to God for all His blessings on both the family and on the nation. Its day, however, has varied in the past from time to time and from place to place. It was apparently first observed by the Pilgrims at Plymouth in 1621, after their first harvest, and then was intermittently observed during and after the Revolutionary War, especially noteworthy when President Washington appointed a Day of Thanksgiving on Thursday, November 26, in 1789. In recent times, it has become a time for family reunions and for religious services.

LABORERS TOGETHER WITH GOD

"For we are laborers together with God: ye are God's husbandry, ye are God's building" (1 Cor. 3:9).

Labor Day was established as a national holiday in this country in 1894 in order to celebrate the important part played by workers in the development of the nation. The first labor laws were passed only in 1802 and the first labor unions formed only in 1825, both being in England.

God has been working since the beginning. After finishing His work of creating and making all things (Gen. 2:1–3), He has ever since been "upholding all things by the word of his power" (Heb. 1:3). Furthermore, although God "rested" from His work of creation, He very soon began His great work of reconciliation, and both His work of conservation and His work of reconciliation still continue today. Jesus said, therefore, "My Father worketh hitherto, and I work" (John 5:17).

It is in this great work of reconciliation that we have the high privilege of being "laborers together with God." Paul has reminded us that God "hath reconciled us to himself by Jesus Christ, and hath given to us the ministry of reconciliation" (2 Cor. 5:18).

As farm laborers have worked in the fields and vineyards of the world to sow and water and reap, and as construction laborers have worked to build the structures and machinery of the world, so we who belong to Christ have the responsibility to produce spiritual fruit in our lives and the lives of others (John 15:16) and to add spiritual building blocks to God's "holy temple in the Lord" (Eph. 2:21).

Instead of the primeval curse, therefore, our "labor in the Lord" (Rom. 16:12) becomes a blessing when we "do it heartily, as to the Lord" (Col. 3:23). Christ promises, when He comes again, "to give every man according as his work shall be" (Rev. 22:12).

WORK IS A GIFT of God and will be eternal. It is appropriate, however, to invent and use labor-saving devices when appropriate and also to pay appropriate wages for work. The labor movement has been valuable in many ways in helping to attain these ends. In any case, God has ordained that "Six days shalt thou labor, and do all thy work" (Exod. 20:9), with one day out of the seven-day week set aside for rest and worship.

GOING FORTH
TO WORK

"Man goeth forth unto his work and to his labor until the evening"
(Ps. 104:23).

This verse is a capsule job description of God's plan for man after the Flood. Psalm 104 first deals with the initial creation (verses 1–5), then with the Flood (verses 6–9), and finally with God's providential provisions for the life of the post-Flood world — plant life, animal life, and human life (verses 10–35).

As in the beginning with Adam (Gen. 3:17–19), man's life would continue to be structured around his personal labor to provide for himself and the needs of his family. It is thus ordained by God for man to labor in some honorable vocation, but disgraceful for him not to work as long as he is able. "The desire of the slothful killeth him; for his hands refuse to labor" (Prov. 21:25). Christians in particular are exhorted to be "not slothful in business; fervent in spirit; serving the Lord" (Rom. 12:11). The apostle Paul commanded "that if any would not work, neither should he eat" (2 Thess. 3:10).

It is significant that the modern recognition of the dignity and importance of labor largely originated in Christian nations, especially England and America. Labor Day itself seems to have started with an annual parade in New York City back in the 1880s, organized by an early labor union, the Knights of Labor. Like most holidays, however, its original purpose now seems to have become largely taken over by commercialization and recreation. The former six-day, dawn-to-dusk work week has given way to the 40-hour (or less) work week and the TGIF syndrome.

This attitude should not characterize Christians. The job assignment God has given each of us to do should be done "heartily, as to the Lord, and not unto man" (Col. 3:23), "forasmuch as ye know that your labor is not in vain in the Lord" (1 Cor. 15:58).

WORKING
AND EATING

"This we commanded you, that if any would not work, neither should he eat. For we hear that there are some which walk among you disorderly, working not at all, but are busybodies. Now them that are such we command and exhort by our Lord Jesus Christ, that with quietness they work, and eat their own bread" (2 Thess. 3:10–12).

The command to work is even in the Ten Commandments! We think of the Fourth Commandment as ordaining a rest day, but it also commands six work days. "Six days shalt thou labor, and do all thy work" (Exod. 20:9).

The Apostle did not say that the one who *could not* work should not eat, but the one who *would not* work. Those able to work are, in fact, encouraged "to give to him that needeth" (Eph. 4:28).

Even before sin entered the world (after God had placed Adam in the Garden of Eden), He commanded him "to dress it and to keep it" (Gen. 2:15). In the new, perfected earth, it is recorded that "His servants shall serve him" (Rev. 22:3).

Honorable, useful work is eternally pleasing to God. Most people today think of Labor Day merely as a holiday, but its true purpose should be to stress the God-approved value of honest, diligent work.

On the other hand, laziness and willing idleness are dishonoring to the Lord. God has saved us by grace, apart from works, but it is "unto good works" (Eph. 2:10). Idle hands easily become the devil's workshop, as the old saying goes, and so does an idle tongue. Work with quietness; "study to be quiet, and to do your own business" (1 Thess. 4:11). Don't let yourself become a meddling, officious busybody, minding other people's affairs while neglecting your own responsibilities. These instructions are given by Paul for two reasons: that our personal needs be met and our Christian testimony be not hindered (1 Thess. 4:12).

LABOR
OR SERVICE?

"Six days thou shalt labor, and do all thy work" (Deut. 5:13).

The term "labor" to many seems to connote drudgery or routine, repetitive, demeaning toil. As used here in the fourth of God's Ten Commandments, however, the Hebrew word *abad* means rather to "serve" and is so translated 214 times in the King James. Only one other time is it translated "labor," and that is in the first rendering of the commandments (Exod. 20:9). Thus, the command could well be read: "Six days shalt thou *serve*."

Furthermore, the word for "work" (Hebrew, *melakah*) does not denote servile labor, but "deputyship," or "stewardship." The one whom we are to serve or act as deputy for, of course, is God himself, when we do our work. In the ultimate and very real sense, the Lord is our employer, and we serve Him, not man. Therefore, "whatsoever ye do, do it heartily, as to the Lord, and not unto men" (Col. 3:23). Every honest occupation, if carried out for the Lord's sake and to His glory, is "divine service," and every Christian who holds this perspective on his or her work (be it preaching, or bookkeeping, or homemaking, or whatever) is in the Christian ministry — for "ministry" simply means "service."

Note also that God has ordained not a four-day or five-day work week: "Six days thou shalt labor, and do all thy work" He says, thus commemorating the six days in which He worked in the beginning, "for in six days the LORD made heaven and earth" (Exod. 31:17).

One day, Lord willing, we shall hear Him say, "Well done, thou good and faithful servant . . . enter thou into the joy of thy Lord" (Matt. 25:21). Then, throughout the ages to come, "His servants shall serve him" (Rev. 22:3) with everlasting joy.

THE LABORER
AND HIS WAGES

"For the scripture saith, Thou shalt not muzzle the ox that treadeth out the corn. And, The laborer is worthy of his reward" (1 Tim. 5:18).

This seemingly rather inconspicuous verse in Paul's personal letter to his young follower Timothy is actually quite significant on several counts. It is fitting for Labor Day, of course, because it confirms that any one who "labors" deserves respect and appropriate pay.

The previous verse (verse 17) shows that this principle applies to all those "elders," whether laboring in "ruling" or "in the word and doctrine" as deserving of "double honor" if they "rule well." The word translated "honor" is often translated "price," so could refer here either to respect or monetary remuneration or both. It also confirms, parenthetically, as it were, that God cares about His animal creation (note also Prov. 12:10; Num. 22:21–34; Job 39).

Perhaps most significantly of all, it quotes two seemingly inconspicuous verses (one in Deut. 25:4, the other in Luke 10:7), calling both of them "scripture" and citing them as justifying adequate financial support for those who devote their time and abilities to the Lord's work.

The quote from Luke 10:7 is as follows: "And in the same house remain, eating and drinking such things as they give: for the laborer is worthy of his hire." These were among the instructions given by Christ as He sent out the 70 to witness to the people of Israel.

Paul clearly considered that Christ's words, as written by Luke, were Scripture on the same basis as the words written by Moses in Deuteronomy. Paul's words were themselves later called "Scriptures" like those of the Old Testament by Peter. We can confidently assume, therefore, that both the Old and New Testament writings were accepted by the apostles as the authoritative Word of God.

Man and His Labor

"Man goeth forth unto his work and to his labor until the evening" (Ps. 104:23).

The 104th Psalm is a beautiful psalm of creation and the Flood, supplemented by God's providential care of His creatures in the post-Flood world. Our text makes man's activity seem almost incidental in the grand scope of God's activities on behalf of His whole creation.

Nevertheless, it reminds us of God's first great commission to mankind concerning that creation. "Have dominion . . . over all the earth . . . to dress it and to keep it" (Gen. 1:26–2:15). This primeval mandate, though still in effect as man's stewardship responsibility for the earth and its creatures, has been seriously impacted by sin and the curse. "Cursed is the ground for thy sake," God told Adam; "in the sweat of thy face shalt thou eat bread" (Gen. 3:17, 19).

So it is that men (women, too!) must work, and the work often is laborious and stressful and unappreciated. Yet the divine rule is "that ye study to be quiet, and to do your own business, and to work with your own hands . . . that ye may walk honestly . . . and that ye may have lack of nothing" (1 Thess. 4:11–12). "For . . . if any would not work, neither should he eat" (2 Thess. 3:10).

Thus labor is necessary, even for those who don't know the Lord. It is far better if we work, not just to earn a living, but to please the Lord. "Whatsoever ye do, do it heartily, as to the Lord, and not unto men" (Col. 3:23).

Whatever our job may be (assuming it is an honorable occupation), it can be regarded as serving Christ and as helping to fulfill His primeval-dominion commandment, and even as helping to lead others to know Him. Therefore, whether the work is easy or hard, we should be "always abounding in the work of the Lord . . . your labor is not in vain in the Lord" (1 Cor. 15:58).

BE
DILIGENT

"And beside this, giving all diligence, add to your faith virtue; and to virtue knowledge" (2 Pet. 1:5).

The importance of diligence is urged by Peter as basic in the development of the seven other virtues listed by him — that is, virtue, knowledge, temperance, patience, godliness, brotherly kindness, charity — as vital additions to our faith. Diligence is seldom considered as a particular Christian attribute, but it is essential if we really desire to develop the other Christian virtues in our lives. They do not come by wishing or hoping. Peter also exhorts us to "give diligence to make your calling and election sure" (2 Pet. 1:10), and then to "be diligent that ye may be found of him in peace, without spot, and blameless" (2 Pet. 3:14).

Essentially the same Greek word is also translated "study" and "labor" and "endeavor." Paul commands: "Study to show thyself approved unto God, a workman that needeth not to be ashamed, rightly dividing the word of truth"(2 Tim. 2:15). He beseeches us always to be "endeavoring to keep the unity of the Spirit in the bond of peace" (Eph. 4:3). We are even told to "labor therefore to enter into that rest" (Heb. 4:11).

There are many other such exhortations in which Christian diligence is urged or shown in reference to other Christian virtues. There is one key verse, however, in which diligence itself is commanded as a Christian duty: "Not slothful in business; fervent in spirit; serving the Lord" (Rom. 12:11). Here the word "business" is the same as "diligence." That is, each Christian is commanded to "be diligent in diligence!"

Christian salvation is received solely by grace through faith. The Christian life, however, demands diligence. Can we not, as our text commands, give all diligence in our service to the Lord who gave His life for us?

WORKING
BY FAITH

"So when even was come, the lord of the vineyard saith unto his steward, Call the laborers, and give them their hire, beginning from the last unto the first" (Matt. 20:8).

This parable has long caused perplexity, not only among the workers in the parable, but also among readers ever since. Why would the Lord teach that wages paid for a given type of work should be the same for 1 hour's work as for 12? His only explanation was that it was the owner's right to do what he wanted with his own money, and that "the last shall be first, and the first last" (Matt. 20:16).

He also reminded the complaining workmen that he had fulfilled his contract with them. Early in the morning, this group had negotiated their own terms with him, and "he had agreed with the laborers for a penny a day" (Matt. 20:2). Those he hired later had said nothing about pay, being glad to work, and willing to trust the lord of the vineyard to treat them fairly. This probably means that the owner had first approached the early morning workers on the same basis, but they were unwilling to work without a contract, negotiating their own terms.

This is the difference. The first group insisted on a firm contract, and the owner therefore insisted on honoring it. The others worked by faith, trusting in the lord of the vineyard, knowing him to be a man of integrity and justice. Furthermore, they would have been willing to work all day long on this same basis, but they had no opportunity. They needed the job, and the owner, knowing their needs and their willing hearts, decided to pay them on the basis of what they would have done, had they had the opportunity.

In any case, the parable surely teaches us that our heavenly rewards are not based on *quantity* of services rendered, but on *quality*, with full account taken of opportunities, motivation, and trust in the Lord.

WORTHY OF
HIS HIRE

"And in the same house remain, eating and drinking such things as they give: for the laborer is worthy of his hire. Go not from house to house" (Luke 10:7).

These words of the Lord Jesus are of special significance in a number of ways. They were part of His commissioning instructions, as it were, as He was sending out His disciples on what could be considered the first Christian missionary journey, in preparation perhaps for the worldwide mission on which He would be sending them soon. As such, there are a number of principles that could be applicable to all who "labor" for the Lord.

They were not to go begging for support "from house to house," but they were free to accept such help as was offered. It was not their responsibility to *win* converts, but simply to *witness*, with the responsibility to believe resting entirely on the hearers. For those who would *not* receive them, the disciples' remaining responsibility was simply to warn them of judgment to come (see Luke 10:10–16).

Another important general principle is that those who are called to full-time service for the Lord are worthy of support by those they serve, rather than having also to be holding down a secular job to make a living. That support should be adequate, but need not be lavish.

One other unique aspect of this verse is that it is the *only* verse in the New Testament which is later quoted as Scripture in the New Testament. "For the scripture saith. . . . The laborer is worthy of his reward" (1 Tim. 5:18). One of the purposes of setting aside a holiday called Labor Day is to recognize the value of honest, useful work. Even those Christians in so-called secular labor can rightfully regard it as "to the Lord" (Col. 3:23), but it is especially appropriate to honor those who, like "the beloved Persis," have "labored much in the Lord" (Rom. 16:12).

LABOR
AND PROFIT

"Then I looked on all the works that my hands had wrought, and on the labor that I had labored to do: and, behold, all was vanity and vexation of spirit, and there was no profit under the sun" (Eccles. 2:11).

One of the inequities of human life seems to be that there is no dependable relation between the diligence with which one labors and the reward he receives for that labor. Some men may work hard all their lives, yet live in poverty. The "idle rich," on the other hand, may inherit their wealth and see it multiply abundantly, simply on the interest received from investments. What sort of "profit" should be assigned to "labor," and who should receive that profit is a problem that perpetually vexes economists and has even led to violent revolutions.

The trouble is that perfect equity can never be achieved in such matters while man's entire dominion is in bondage to sin and death, under God's curse (Gen. 2:17–19). As long as one's goals and motives in working are only "under the sun," there is bound to be "vanity and vexation of spirit," no matter what his current economic and social status may be. The accounts are not to be settled in the fallible ledgers kept here on earth, but in God's books.

"Labor not for the meat which perisheth," said the Lord, "but for that meat which endureth unto everlasting life" (John 6:27). It was to bondslaves he was speaking when Paul said, "Whatsoever ye do, do it heartily, as to the Lord, and not unto men; Knowing that of the Lord ye shall receive the reward of the inheritance: for ye serve the Lord Christ" (Col. 3:23–24).

It is important to remember that, when all accounts are settled at His Judgment seat, the "profit" we receive is not based on quantity, but quality, of services rendered. "Every man's work shall be made manifest: for the day shall declare it . . . and the fire shall try every man's work of what sort it is" (1 Cor. 3:13).

Not "how much," but "what sort"! There is little profit under the sun, but if we are "abounding in the work of the Lord . . . your labor is not in vain in the Lord" (1 Cor. 15:58).

LABOR DAY
A "HOLY" DAY?

"Let no man therefore judge you in meat, or in drink, or in respect of an holyday, or of the new moon, or of the sabbath days" (Col. 2:16).

This is the only verse in the New Testament that has any reference to holidays (at one time considered "holy days"). However, the Greek word so translated does occur there quite often, being rendered elsewhere always by its correct meaning of "feasts."

Such "holy days" in the Old Testament economy normally required "no servile work" to be done on those days, and were usually associated with a special "feast" of some deep spiritual significance. They certainly were not holidays in the modern sense, devoted mostly to pleasure.

In fact, it is perhaps significant that neither holidays nor vacations are mentioned in the Bible at all. The weekly Sabbath "rest" day is, of course, frequently emphasized. One day in seven has always been observed as a day to rest from labor and to remember our Creator. However, the other six days were to be spent working. Many can still remember when the norm was a six-day work week.

Not so now. Many complain about even a five-day week, and "TGIF" is a common feeling as the weekend approaches. "Labor" Day is now a day mainly for fun, but it might be a good day for Christians to thank God for the privilege of work and doing that work "heartily, as to the Lord" (Col. 3:23). Our work, whatever it may be, can become a real testimony for (or, sadly, against) the Lord whom we profess to serve.

In the ages to come, there will still be work to do for the Lord. In that day, it is promised that "His servants shall serve him" (Rev. 22:3). Therefore, we should be "abounding in the work of the Lord" right now. It will not be "in vain" (1 Cor. 15:58).

THE
PILGRIMS

"Peter, an apostle of Jesus Christ, to the strangers scattered throughout Pontus, Galatia, Cappadocia, Asia, and Bithynia" (1 Pet. 1:1).

These "strangers" to whom Peter wrote his two epistles were actually "pilgrims." He used the same Greek word (*parepidemos*) in 1 Peter 2:11: "Dearly beloved, I beseech you as strangers and *pilgrims*, abstain from fleshly lusts." The word means a resident foreigner, and its only other New Testament usage is in Hebrews 11:13, speaking of the ancient patriarchs, who "confessed that they were strangers and *pilgrims* on the earth."

We give honor on Thanksgiving Day to the American "pilgrims," as they called themselves (thinking of these very verses), who left their homelands in order better to serve God in a foreign land. The "pilgrims" to whom Peter was writing likewise had been "scattered abroad" for their faith (note Acts 8:4).

For that matter, every born-again believer in the Lord Jesus Christ is really just a pilgrim here on earth, ambassadors for Christ in a foreign land. "For our conversation is in heaven" (Phil. 3:20). That is, we are citizens of heaven (the Greek word translated "conversation" in this verse is *politeuma*, meaning "a community" or "citizenship"), and are here only for a time to serve our Lord until He calls us home.

While we are here, we may endure many trials and sorrows, just as did those Massachusetts pilgrims, but He nevertheless supplies our needs — just as He did for them — and we ought to abound in thanksgiving, as they did.

Of all people in the history of the world, none have more cause for thanksgiving than American Christians. Therefore, since we are "enriched in every thing," through our Savior, this "causeth through us thanksgiving to God" (2 Cor. 9:11), and we should be "abounding therein with thanksgiving" (Col. 2:7).

THE BIBLE FREQUENTLY emphasizes the importance of praise and thanks. This nation has much reason for praise and thanksgiving, for God has blessed us perhaps more than any other. "Be thankful unto Him, and bless His name. For the Lord is good; His mercy is everlasting; and His truth endureth to all generations" (Ps. 100:4–5).

THANKSGIVING
IN THE BIBLE

"Being enriched in every thing to all bountifulness, which causeth through us thanksgiving to God" (2 Cor. 9:11).

The themes of praise and thanksgiving are very prominent throughout Scripture. The word "praise" and its derivatives occur over 330 times, and "thanks," with its derivatives, over 150 times. When applied to our relation to God, "thanks" are given to Him for what He has done for us, and "praise" for who He is and what He has done for the whole creation. If frequency of occurrence were an indicator, we might conclude that thanksgiving is important and praise-giving is twice as important!

In any case, every Christian believer has a tremendous amount to be thankful for. As in our text, we have been "enriched in every thing to all bountifulness," and it is sad to hear so many complaints and laments coming from Christians who feel they deserve more and better than they have already received from God's good hand.

We are told that the Lord Jesus, instituting the Lord's Supper, gave thanks, all the while knowing that the very elements He was blessing spoke of His body that would soon be broken and His blood that would soon be shed. No wonder, therefore, that the apostle Paul reminds us, "In every thing give thanks: for this is the will of God in Christ Jesus concerning you" (1 Thess. 5:18).

Whether in bountifulness of material blessing or in the invaluable school of suffering and discipline, we can please God by a thankful heart and life. A key evidence that a Christian is truly "filled with the Spirit" is that he or she is habitually "giving thanks always for all things unto God and the Father in the name of our Lord Jesus Christ" (Eph. 5:18, 20). May God's Spirit "cause through us thanksgiving to God!"

THANKS BE UNTO GOD

"But thanks be to God, which giveth us the victory through our Lord Jesus Christ" (1 Cor. 15:57).

There are innumerable things for which we could — and should — give thanks to God. There are three notable gifts mentioned by Paul in his letters to the Corinthians, in which He was led to use this particular exclamation: "Thanks be to God." We shall do well to look at these three great blessings and then, like Paul, pour out our own thanks to God for them!

The first is in our text above, giving thanks for God's gift of victory. What victory is that? "Death is swallowed up in victory" (1 Cor. 15:54), and death has lost its terrible sting for the believer, for Christ conquered death forever when He died for our sins and rose again.

The second is similar, yet goes beyond even the first gift: "Now thanks be unto God, which always causeth us to triumph in Christ, and maketh manifest the savour of his knowledge by us in every place" (2 Cor. 2:14). Not only victory over death, but victory in life! By the indwelling presence of the Spirit of Christ, we are enabled to triumph over circumstances and "show forth the praises of him who hath called [us] out of darkness into his marvelous light" (1 Pet. 2:9).

The greatest gift of all is Christ himself! Therefore, we join with the apostle Paul as he exclaims, "Thanks be unto God for his unspeakable gift" (2 Cor. 9:15). "For God so loved the world, that he gave his only begotten Son, that whosoever believeth in him should not perish, but have everlasting life" (John 3:16). The value of this gift is beyond language to describe, "unspeakable and full of glory" (1 Pet. 1:8).

The Lord Jesus Christ is both our Creator and Savior, giving us triumphant peace and joy in life, and eternal victory over death. Thanks be unto God!

THANKS FOR
CHRISTIAN FRIENDS

"We give thanks to God always for you all, making mention of you in our prayers" (1 Thess. 1:2).

We all have much to be thankful for. It is certainly appropriate to give audible thanks for our daily bread, whether in private, at a family meal, or in public at a fine restaurant. In fact, Jesus set the example. When He miraculously fed the multitude beside the sea of Galilee, He began with a prayer of thanksgiving: "He took the seven loaves and the fishes, and gave thanks, and brake them. . . . And they did all eat, and were filled" (Matt. 15:36–37).

It is good to give thanks for our food and shelter and clothing, but the blessing of having Christian friends is even more thankworthy. Possibly the first letter to the Thessalonians was Paul's first Spirit-inspired letter to Christian friends, and Paul began with a testimony of thankfulness to God for them (see text above).

When Paul wrote to the Philippians, he began similarly: "I thank my God upon every remembrance of you" (Phil. 1:3), and to the Colossians, he started the same way: "We give thanks to God and the Father of our Lord Jesus Christ, praying always for you" (Col. 1:3). Paul expressed the same thoughts when he wrote his epistle to the church at Corinth. "I thank my God always on your behalf, for the grace of God which is given you by Jesus Christ" (1 Cor. 1:4).

Even when writing to the Christians at Rome, whom he had not yet met personally, he wrote, "First, I thank my God through Jesus Christ for you all" (Rom. 1:8). He also thanked God for his personal friends Timothy (2 Tim. 1:3) and Philemon (verse 4).

This writer has lived in nine different cities and can thank God for Christian friends in all of them. What a blessing to have such friends, and how fitting it is to give God special thanks for them at this time.

Remember
His Benefits

"Bless the LORD, O my soul, and forget not all his benefits" (Ps. 103:2).

The benefits of the Lord are, indeed, great and marvelous, and it would be an act of ingratitude not to remember and appreciate them. Note the following partial list in this psalm:

Forgiveness. "Who forgiveth all thine iniquities" (Ps. 103:3). God forgives *all!* He "cleanseth us from all sin" (1 John 1:7).

Healing. "Who healeth all thy diseases" (Ps. 103:3). The greatest and ultimate disease is that of aging and death, but one day, "there shall be no more death" (Rev. 21:4).

Redemption. "Who redeemeth thy life from destruction" (Ps. 103:4; see also 1 Pet. 1:18–19).

Glorification. "Who crowneth thee with lovingkindness and tender mercies" (Ps. 103:4).

Provision. "Who satisfieth thy mouth with good things" (Ps. 103:5; see also James 1:17).

Strength. "Thy youth is renewed like the eagle's" (Ps. 103:5).

Protection. "The Lord executeth righteousness and judgment for all that are oppressed" (Ps. 103:6).

The greatest benefit of all, of course, is the gift of salvation, by the mercy of God. Note the testimonies of God's mercy:

"Who crowneth thee with lovingkindness and tender *mercies*" (Ps. 103:4). "The LORD is *merciful* and gracious, slow to anger, and plenteous in mercy" (verse 8). "For as the heaven is high above the earth, so great is His *mercy* toward them that fear Him" (verse 11). "But the *mercy* of the LORD is from everlasting to everlasting upon them that fear Him" (verse 17).

Infinite as the universe, enduring as eternity — these are the dimensions of God's mercy! "As far as the east is from the west, so far hath He removed our transgressions from us" (verse 12). No wonder this great psalm both begins and ends with the inspiring exhortation: "Bless the LORD, O my soul!"

In Everything
Give Thanks

"Although the fig tree shall not blossom, neither shall fruit be in the vines; the labor of the olive shall fail, and the fields shall yield no meat; the flock shall be cut off from the fold, and there shall be no herd in the stalls: Yet I will rejoice in the Lord, I will joy in the God of my salvation" (Hab. 3:17–18).

I t is easy to be happy and cheerful in times of prosperity, when one has all the comforts of an affluent lifestyle, and everything seems to be going well. The testing times come, however, when these material comforts are somehow taken away, and one feels defeated and all alone.

Except for God! Whatever else may fail, God "will never leave thee, nor forsake thee" (Heb. 13:5). Since we still have the Lord (assuming we have trusted Him for forgiveness and salvation, through Christ), we can always "rejoice in the Lord . . . in the God of my salvation."

Job, for example, lost all his possessions, then his children, finally his health, and even his wife turned against him. Yet he could say, "The Lord gave, and the Lord hath taken away; blessed be the name of the Lord" (Job 1:21).

God has commanded the Christian, "In every thing give thanks: for this is the will of God in Christ Jesus concerning you" (1 Thess. 5:18). Not for everything, but *in* everything!

This has always been one of the greatest testimonies a Christian can give to an unbeliever — the testimony of a life rejoicing in God's salvation even in the midst of trouble. This was the example of Christ himself, "who for the joy that was set before him endured the cross, despising the shame, and is set down at the right hand of the throne of God" (Heb. 12:2). "For our light affliction, which is but for a moment, worketh for us a far more exceeding and eternal weight of glory" (2 Cor. 4:17).

THANKS FOR EVERYTHING

"Giving thanks always for all things unto God and the Father in the name of our Lord Jesus Christ" (Eph. 5:20).

Being thankful for everything that happens in his or her life to a Christian believer is listed in this section of Paul's letter to the Ephesians as one of the evidences that a Christian is indeed "filled with the Spirit" (Eph. 5:18).

That is not all. Not only for everything, but in everything, we should give thanks to God. "In every thing give thanks: for this is the will of God in Christ Jesus concerning you" (1 Thess. 5:18).

These two commands are easy to obey when the living is easy, as the song says, though we might easily forget to do so, but when the Lord is allowing us to hurt for a while, thanksgiving becomes hard. It is hard while we are experiencing the difficulty and just as hard when it has passed with no relief in sight. The two small prepositions "in" and "for" are different in New Testament Greek as well as in modern English, and God really wants us to learn how to thank Him both during and after the hard experience.

Because He has allowed it for a good purpose! The apostle James urges us to "count it all joy when ye fall into divers temptations" (that is, "various testings"); "Knowing this, that the trying of your faith worketh patience. But let patience have her perfect work, that ye may be perfect and entire, wanting nothing" (James 1:3–4). Paul says that we can even "glory in tribulations also: knowing that tribulation worketh patience; And patience, experience; and experience, hope: And hope maketh not ashamed; because the love of God is shed abroad in our hearts by the Holy Ghost which is given unto us" (Rom. 5:3–5). Patience and real love will come to characterize a habitually thankful Christian.

SING AND
GIVE THANKS

"Sing unto the LORD, O ye saints of his, and give thanks at the remembrance of his holiness" (Ps. 30:4).

When we do remember God's holiness and then remember how the mighty seraphim in the heavenly temple are continually crying out "Holy, holy, holy, is the Lord of hosts" (Isa. 6:3), and then further remember the prophet's prayer acknowledging to God that "Thou art of purer eyes than to behold evil, and canst not look on iniquity" (Hab. 1:13), and then still further remember that, as Paul said, "For I know that in me (that is, in my flesh,) dwelleth no good thing" (Rom. 7:18), we can only marvel at the infinite mercy and grace of God. He has not only forgiven our sins, saved our souls, and promised us eternal life, but "daily loadeth us with benefits, even the God of our salvation" (Ps. 68:19). What can we do except to perpetually "sing unto the Lord . . . and give thanks" as David exhorts us in our text for today.

How can this be? A God who is too pure and holy even to "look on iniquity," yet promises unworthy creatures such as us that "goodness and mercy shall follow [us] all the days of [our lives]: and [we] will dwell in the house of the Lord for ever" (Ps. 23:6). How *can* that be?

This could *not* be, of course, were it not for the incredible love of God in Christ, who "hath once suffered for sins, the just for the unjust, that he might bring us to God" (1 Pet. 3:18). "The chastisement of our peace was upon him; and with his stripes we are healed" (Isa. 53:5). "While we were yet sinners, Christ died for us" (Rom. 5:8).

Therefore: "Be ye thankful . . . singing with grace in your hearts to the Lord. And whatsoever ye do in word or deed, do all in the name of the Lord Jesus, giving thanks to God and the Father by him" (Col. 3:15–17).

Thanks for the Greatest Gift

"Thanks be unto God for his unspeakable gift" (2 Cor. 9:15).

We who have known and sought to follow the Lord for many years have received many, many blessings for which to thank Him. "Blessed be the Lord, who daily loadeth us with benefits" (Ps. 68:19), we can pray again and again.

There is one blessing which is so great that it cannot even be put into words — it is *unspeakable!* That gift is so great that when we try to comprehend it, the sense of awe and gratitude becomes so overwhelming (or at least *should* become so overwhelming) that our joy is also unspeakable and indescribable! That gift is the gift of the Lord Jesus Christ as our Redeemer and Savior, "Whom having not seen, ye love; in whom, though now ye see him not, yet believing ye rejoice with joy unspeakable and full of glory" (1 Pet. 1:8).

It is significant that the Greek word translated "unspeakable" occurs only these two times in the entire New Testament. God's unspeakable gift *to* us produces unspeakable joy *in* us. We who deserve nothing but eternal separation *from* God in hell, instead will enjoy eternal life *with* God in heaven, and all because of that amazing and truly inexpressible gift!

To think that the mighty Creator, God the Son, would not only humble himself to become His own creature, man, but then also suffer the unimaginable agony of the Cross and separation from God the Father in order to deliver us from the just penalty of sin! This act speaks of such love and grace that all we can do is whisper softly, "Thank you, Lord, for this unspeakable gift," and then shout it over and over again in our hearts wherever we go, and share its unspeakable joy and blessing with whomever will listen to its message. "The LORD hath done great things for us; whereof we are glad" (Ps. 126:3). Thank You, Lord!

THANKSGIVING IN HEAVEN

"And the four and twenty elders, which sat before God on their seats [thrones], fell upon their faces, and worshipped God, Saying, We give thee thanks, O Lord God Almighty, which art, and wast, and art to come; because thou hast taken to thee thy great power, and hast reigned" (Rev. 11:16–17).

This is the final reference in the Bible to the giving of thanks. It records a scene in heaven where the 24 elders, representing all redeemed believers, are thanking God that His primeval promise of restoration and victory is about to be fulfilled. The petition, "thy kingdom come" (Matt. 6:10), is now ready to be answered.

Similarly, the final reference to the offering of praise is also set in heaven. "And a voice came out of the throne, saying, 'Praise our God, all ye his servants, and ye that fear him, both small and great.' And I heard as it were the voice of a great multitude, and as the voice of many waters, and as the voice of mighty thunderings, saying, Alleluia: for the Lord God omnipotent reigneth" (Rev. 19:5–6).

The word "alleluia" is the same as the Hebrew word "hallelujah," meaning, "Praise ye the Lord!" Thus, the joyful notes of praise for who He is and thankfulness for what He has done will resound through heaven when Christ returns. Then, forevermore, the very lives of all His saints will be perpetual testimonies of thanksgiving and praise.

This is our destiny, if we have received Christ by faith as Savior and Lord. It is important that our lives even now begin to reflect such a character, that we may be the better prepared as the day approaches. "In every thing give thanks: for this is the will of God in Christ Jesus concerning you" (1 Thess. 5:18). "By him therefore let us offer the sacrifice of praise to God continually, that is, the fruit of our lips giving thanks to his name" (Heb. 13:15).

Chapter VII

Key Days in American History

Every nation has had one or more key days in their history, and our nation is certainly no exception. Some of these have been included in Chapter V ("Patriotic Holidays"), and there are many more, too many in fact to include in this compilation of brief Bible studies.

However, three such days really must be included. One is Columbus Day, recognizing the supposed actual "discovery" of America by Christopher Columbus back in 1492, almost three centuries before the formal organization of the United States of America. Once the USA became a free and independent country, its history has been especially developed around two great wars — the American Revolution and the American Civil War. The presidents especially involved in these two periods of American history were George Washington, who became our first president, and Abraham Lincoln, president of the Union at the time of the War Between the States.

Because of their inspired leaders' help during these two periods, Washington and Lincoln were long honored with national holidays on their respective birthdays (Lincoln on February 12, Washington on February 22). However, there have been other very worthy presidents in our over two centuries of history, so these two holidays are currently consolidated into one holiday called Presidents' Day, usually observed on a Monday between February 12 and 22.

The most costly and devastating war in our history, however, occurred more recently, while F.D. Roosevelt was president. This war, now known as World War II, began on December 7, 1941, when Japanese airplanes bombed the U.S. Pacific Fleet in the famous Pearl Harbor in Honolulu, Hawaii, severely crippling it. War was immediately declared (on Germany and Italy, as well as Japan) and continued until victory was finally achieved over all three in 1945. Since that time, December 7 has been observed as Pearl Harbor Day by our country — as a time of remembrance and rededication.

THE CIRCLE OF THE EARTH

"It is he that sitteth upon the circle of the earth, and the inhabitants thereof are as grasshoppers; that stretcheth out the heavens as a curtain, and spreadeth them out as a tent to dwell in" (Isa. 40:22).

The discovery that the world is round is considered one of man's greatest scientific discoveries, and is often attributed to Christopher Columbus. Columbus was, indeed, a great and courageous thinker and explorer, as well as a Bible-believing Christian, but it was not really he who discovered America or who first proved the world was round. The American Indians reached both North and South America, migrating out from the regions near Mount Ararat after the great Flood, thousands of years before Columbus or the Vikings or any other early explorers did.

As far as the sphericity of the earth is concerned, the "flat earth" myth of the Middle Ages was not the belief of many scholars of antiquity. The Bible, in particular, never hints of a drop-off point at the earth's edge, or any such notion as that. Its few references to "the four corners" of the earth (e.g., Isa. 11:12) literally mean "the four quarters of the earth" — that is, the four quadrants of the compass.

In our text for the day, the word for "circle" is translated "compass" in Proverbs 8:27. "[God] set a compass upon the face of the depth" (same as "deep," referring to the ocean surface). Another occurrence is Job 26:10: "He hath compassed the waters with bounds, until the day and night come to an end." One other usage is in Job 22:14: "[God] walketh in the circuit of heaven." All of these passages are best understood in terms of a spherical earth, with its basic shape at sea level determined by its ocean surface as controlled by gravity, all surrounded by a great celestial "sphere" of the heavens. The Hebrew word itself (*khug*) basically means a circle. Any vertical cross section through the earth's center is a "great circle," of course, with any apparently "straight" line projected by it on the ocean surface actually representing an arc of such a circle.

This is only one of many "pre-scientific" insights of the Bible written by divine inspiration long before the rise of modern science.

ALTHOUGH CHRISTOPHER COLUMBUS was not really the first to discover America, he was a sincere Christian and a brave and capable explorer. It is surely appropriate to recognize and honor him with a special day.

COLUMBUS
AND THE DOVE

*"And the dove came in to him in the evening; and, lo, in her mouth
was an olive leaf pluckt off: so Noah knew that the waters were abated
from off the earth"* (Gen. 8:11).

When the terrible Flood covered the whole earth in the days of
Noah, the record says that "all flesh died that moved upon the
earth . . . all that was in the dry land, died. . . . and Noah only remained
alive, and they that were with him in the ark" (Gen. 7:21–23). Of those
that were with Noah in the ark, the very first occupant to touch down on
the new land surface was the little dove which Noah sent out from the ark
to see if the face of the ground was dry. The dove, so to speak, had "discovered" the new world.

By an interesting circumstance, Columbus was the man God used to
cross the vast waters of the ocean to "discover" the new world of the Ameri-
cas, and the name "Columbus" comes from the Latin word for "dove."
Indeed, Columbus was himself a man of prayer and great faith, and he truly
believed that he was on a God-ordained mission.

Whatever questions can be raised about his later relations with the na-
tives and his other exploits, it does seem clear that God must have protected
and directed his voyage from Spain to America. The subsequent history of
the colonies and especially of our own nation, so greatly blessed and used
of God to spread the gospel of Christ worldwide, surely is evidence enough
of that fact.

In a sense, we ourselves are part of his legacy. Christians are still under
Christ's commission to "be witnesses unto me . . . unto the uttermost part
of the earth" (Acts 1:8). As we go, He says, as to His first disciples: "Behold,
I send you forth as sheep in the midst of wolves: be ye therefore wise as
serpents, and harmless as doves" (Matt. 10:16). As gentle doves, perhaps,
we may be used to bring back an olive leaf, so to speak, to our Savior.

THE DISCOVERY
OF AMERICA

"These are the three sons of Noah: and of them was the whole earth overspread" (Gen. 9:19).

October 12, 1492, is the supposed date when Christopher Columbus "discovered" America, and his story is one of great hardship, Christian faith, and courage, crowned finally with worldwide acclaim.

It is now generally recognized that he was not the first to discover America. Leif Ericson and the Norsemen not only found it before he did, but explored large sections long before Columbus came.

Leif was not even the first. The evidence is mounting that the ancient Phoenicians reached America well before the time of Christ. There is even some evidence that the Egyptians and Chinese may also have come before Leif Ericson. All this is very uncertain, of course.

Even if so, however, they still were not the first. Various tribes of immigrants now known as the American Indians were the real discoverers of America, long before anyone else, probably not too long after the dispersion at the Tower of Babel. Because of the wicked rebellion of all the clans against God, instigated by Nimrod at Babel, the Lord suddenly corrupted the original language into a vast babble of different languages, evidently one per family, "and from thence did the Lord scatter them abroad upon the face of all the earth" (Gen. 11:9). "All the earth," it says, and that would seem to include America.

Some probably traveled by land up through Asia, crossing the Bering Strait land bridge during the Ice Age; some came by sea from Europe or Asia or Africa.

They came in many different tribes and languages and established their "nations" throughout the American continents. There they were ready to greet Leif and Christopher Columbus when these latecomers finally arrived.

THE EARLIEST
EXPLORERS

"Therefore is the name of it called Babel; because the LORD
did there confound the language of all the earth: and from thence
did the LORD scatter them abroad upon the face of all the earth"
(Genesis 11:9).

T he Genesis record makes it abundantly plain that the Noahic deluge was a worldwide cataclysm which destroyed the entire antedi-
luvian human population except those on Noah's ark. From these, the Bible
says, "was the whole earth overspread" (Genesis 9:19). At first, the entire
post-Flood human population wanted to remain in Babel, rejecting God's
command to fill the earth (Genesis 9:1). Therefore, God forced them to
scatter abroad by confusing their languages, thus requiring each family to
fend for itself, wherever its members could find (and defend) a suitable
homeland.

These emigrants thus went out into a truly "new world," exploring its continents and sailing its oceans, some settling in productive regions where
they could eventually develop great civilizations (e.g., Egypt, China),
others continuing to wander until they finally reached the remotest regions
of earth. With all due credit to great explorers like Columbus, neither he
nor Leif Ericson discovered America—the American Indians did!

Today archaeologists are beginning to understand the tremendous
abilities and contributions of these primeval explorers and builders. In
South Africa and Siberia, Peru and the Pacific Islands, ancient sites are being excavated, yielding amazing artifacts of complex cultures almost everywhere. The evolutionary prejudices of modern western anthropologists
and archaeologists have kept these facts unrecognized far too long.

Evolutionists like to imagine that ancient men were ape-like sav-
ages living in gross ignorance. Some of their degenerate progeny may have
come to fit such a description, but the earliest people, immediate descendants of the great patriarch Noah, were great explorers, navigators,
agriculturalists, husbandmen, and builders, and the modern world is
greatly indebted to them for much of its comforts.

Scattered Abroad

"So the LORD scattered them abroad from thence upon the face of all the earth: and they left off to build the city" (Gen. 11:8).

The text verse above is a summary statement of God's judgment at Babel, at which time God confused the languages of the people there and dispersed them throughout the earth. These original nations — all descended from Noah and his three sons — are listed in what is called the "Table of Nations" in Genesis 10. As time went on, the people proliferated into still more nations and languages and migrated still farther from Babel until finally, as the text says, they were scattered "upon the face of all the earth."

Christopher Columbus was a brave explorer and skilled navigator, as well as a diligent Bible student and convinced Christian. However, he did not "discover America," as he is said to have done on October 12 in 1492. Neither did Leif Ericson or any other adventurer whose name has been suggested for this honor.

The *Indians* discovered America! Archaeologists have found Indian artifacts at occupation sites dating well before the time of Christ at many places in America. Wherever these early tribes went, they carried with them the pantheistic religion taught to their ancestors at Babel by Nimrod there in that first great city after the Flood.

Many centuries later, however, there was another great scattering with a much different purpose and motivation. "Therefore they that were scattered abroad went every where preaching the word" (Acts 8:4). This time, it was not a false religion that was being carried with them, but the saving gospel of Christ who had commanded His followers: "Go ye into all the world, and preach the gospel to every creature" (Mark 16:15), even "unto the uttermost part of the earth" (Acts 1:8).

THE
NEW WORLD

"For here have we no continuing city, but we seek one to come"
(Heb. 13:14).

The phrase "the new world" as applied to the two American continents is believed to have been coined by the explorer Amerigo Vespucci, who claimed to have been the first to sight the actual mainland. This is believed to be the chief reason why "America" was named after him rather than Christopher Columbus, who had "discovered" some of the islands of the West Indies just a few years before. (Actually, some of the Norsemen and possibly others "discovered" this new world several centuries before either one — not to mention the American "Indians" who reached the continent much earlier than any of them, probably soon after the dispersion at Babel.)

Columbus himself has many memoria named after him too, of course. Think of the many cities named Columbus or Columbia, as well as the great Columbia River and prestigious Columbia University. Even America itself has been called Columbia in a number of songs and poems.

America was not a "new world" to God! It has been here all along, and we here in America are thankful to be a part of it today.

There is a real new world coming, however! The Old Testament prophet received God's promise long ago. "For behold, I create new heavens and a new earth" (Isa. 65:17). The New Testament prophet John actually described it as seen in a wonderful vision. "And I saw a new heaven and a new earth," he said, and then described some of its beauties (see Rev. 21 and 22).

The apostle Peter transmitted the most wonderful news of all about this new world when he wrote that "we, according to his promise, look for new heavens and a new earth, wherein dwelleth righteousness" (2 Pet. 3:13). All of us, who by faith have been made righteous in Christ, shall live there forever!

Honoring
Our Leaders

"Obey them that have the rule over you, and submit yourselves: for they watch for your souls, as they that must give account, that they may do it with joy, and not with grief: for that is unprofitable for you" (Heb. 13:17).

The text above was written primarily in respect to religious leaders in the churches, but the same exhortation could be applied to political leaders, with the responsibility of governing their respective nations. In the case of our own country, it would surely apply to our presidents, all of whom have professed belief in God and many of whom have been Bible-believing Christians.

Regardless of the government system under which they have come to hold this office, we must remember that "there is no power but of God: the powers that be are ordained of God. Whosoever therefore resisteth the power, resisteth the ordinance of God" (Rom. 13:1-2). Therefore, said Paul to church leaders regarding their members, "Put them in mind to be subject to principalities and powers, to obey magistrates, to be ready to every good work" (Titus 3:1).

Peter said, "Submit yourselves to every ordinance of man for the Lord's sake: whether it be to the king, as supreme; Or unto governors, as unto them that are sent by him for the punishment of evildoers, and for the praise of them that do well. For so is the will of God, that with well doing ye may put to silence the ignorance of foolish men. . . . Fear God. Honor the king" (1 Pet. 2:13–17).

Both Peter and Paul always taught that we should "honor the king," even though both were eventually put to death by him. It is surely appropriate for us today to honor our presidents, especially on this special day. Of course, we must always "obey God rather than men" (Acts 5:29), when such conflicts arise. Remember that they also "must give account" to God some day as they "watch for your souls."

The Righteous
in Authority

When the righteous are in authority, the people rejoice: but when the wicked beareth rule, the people mourn" (Prov. 29:2).

Many can remember when the nation observed holidays on both the birthday of President Lincoln (February 12) and that of President Washington (February 22). These two men were widely revered as our nation's greatest presidents, and their birthdays were patriotic holidays. Modern intellectuals have been actively tarnishing their reputations, while our people have become more and more enamored of recreation, so this situation has now "devolved" into a three-day holiday theoretically honoring all presidents.

We are thankful, of course, that most of our presidents have indeed been God-fearing men. None were atheists and almost all have professed belief in Christ and the Bible. God surely led our founders when they formed our constitutional republic, and our presidents and most other leaders have diligently supported it. Christianity has thrived in our country as a result, and we have become acknowledged everywhere as the world's greatest nation.

Signs of deterioration are abounding, and Christians need to pray. If Paul were here today, he would surely repeat (and slightly rephrase) his first-century admonition to young pastor Timothy: "I exhort therefore, that, first of all, supplications, prayers, intercessions, and giving of thanks, be made for all men; For [presidents], and for all that are in authority; that we may lead a quiet and peaceable life in all godliness and honesty. For this is good and acceptable in the sight of God our Savior; Who will have all men to be saved, and to come unto the knowledge of the truth" (1 Tim. 2:1–3). We can also heed Peter's advice: "Honor all men. Love the brotherhood. Fear God. Honor the [president]" (1 Pet. 2:17).

THIS FAMOUS MONUMENT in the Black Hills of South Dakota honors a number of our most distinguished presidents. Our nation has enjoyed God's blessings in countless ways, no doubt in large measure because of its unique governmental structure as a constitutional republic, frankly recognizing (at least of its founding) its Christian basis.

HONOR TO
WHOM HONOR

"Render therefore to all their dues: tribute to whom tribute is due; custom to whom custom; fear to whom fear; honor to whom honor" (Rom. 13:7).

On Presidents' Day each year, our nation remembers and honors our presidents, especially such great leaders of the past as George Washington and Abraham Lincoln, who played critical roles in the history of our nation. Whether these men were born-again Christians or not is still a matter of controversy, and the same is true of many more recent leaders.

Regardless of that, however, the Bible commands that we honor them, "For there is no power but of God: the powers that be are ordained of God" (Rom. 13:1). If the apostle Paul could write of the pagan, cruel, licentious Roman emperor that "he is the minister of God to thee for good" (Rom. 13:4), then surely this must be true of our own duly elected, nominally Christian leaders today.

We honor them because God has (for reasons that may often be inscrutable to us) placed them in positions of authority. "The most High ruleth in the kingdom of men, and giveth it to whomsoever he will, and setteth up over it the basest of men" (Dan. 4:17).

"Submit yourselves to every ordinance of man for the Lord's sake," we are therefore commanded, "Whether it be to the king, as supreme; Or unto governors" (1 Pet. 2:13–14). We are entitled, of course, also to pursue any avenue provided by these same ordinances for changing them, or for the redress of grievances, or for securing better leaders. When, however, we must choose between obeying a law of God or of human government, "we ought to obey God rather than men" (Acts 5:29). This includes submitting graciously to whatever legal penalty this disobedience entails, "For so is the will of God, that with well doing ye may put to silence the ignorance of foolish men" (1 Pet. 2:15).

Daniel
The President

"It pleased Darius to set over the kingdom an hundred and twenty princes, which should be over the whole kingdom; And over these three presidents; of whom Daniel was first: that the princes might give accounts unto them, and the king should have no damage" (Dan. 6:1–2).

Not many people realize that the godly prophet Daniel was the first president of the great Medo-Persian-Babylonian Empire!

Of course, Daniel's office did not correlate directly with that of an American president, being appointive rather than elective, and being subject to the emperor, but he nevertheless had great authority. Many translations use the word "governor" instead of "president" — the original language was Aramaic in this case, rather than Hebrew.

In any case, Daniel was a God-fearing Hebrew, rather than a Persian or Babylonian, and so soon drew the envy and resentment of the other "presidents" and "princes" of the empire. The only charge they could make against him (there was no hint of scandal or corruption in his character or activities, unlike certain nominally Christians in our own country) was that he was too "religious," worshiping openly the true God of creation instead of the nature-gods of the pagans. "They could find none occasion nor fault; forasmuch as he was faithful, neither was there any error or fault found in him" (Dan. 6:4).

It is sadly true that such a testimony could never have been given concerning any American president, not even Washington or Lincoln, as great and praiseworthy as they were. Nevertheless, God would remind us "that, first of all, supplications, prayers, intercessions, and giving of thanks, be made for all men; For kings, and for all that are in authority; that we may lead a quiet and peaceable life in all godliness and honesty" (1 Tim. 2:1–2).

The Ordinances
of Men

"Submit yourselves to every ordinance of man for the Lord's sake: whether it be to the king, as supreme; Or unto governors, as unto them that are sent by him for the punishment of evildoers, and for the praise of them that do well" (1 Pet. 2:13–14).

The phrase "ordinances of man" literally means "human creations." Since only God can really *create*, that means we must regard laws of legislatures or presidential orders or even kingly decrees as having divine authority. Therefore, in order to maintain a good witness before men, God expects us to submit to all these man-made laws and directives.

That even includes such unpopular laws as speed limits. Christians should not be tax cheats or anything that tends to undermine legitimate authority, and certainly should never break any of the multitude of laws that are based upon or consistent with, the laws or commandments of God. We rightly must honor our leaders, not only great presidents such as Washington and Lincoln, but all who have positions of authority, Remember that "there is no power but of God: the powers that be are ordained of God" (Rom. 13:1), even though there are occasions when (for good and justifiable reasons) God gives power to unworthy men.

Such ungodly leaders will be themselves judged by God in His own way and time. Our job is simply to "render therefore to all their dues: tribute to whom tribute is due; custom to whom custom; fear to whom fear; honor to whom honor" (Rom. 13:7).

The one great exception to this principle, of course, is when their laws go against the laws of God. Then, "we ought to obey God rather than men" (Acts 5:29), and be willing to take the consequences. "If any man suffer as a Christian, let him not be ashamed; but let him glorify God on this behalf" (1 Pet. 4:16).

George
and Abraham

"Let the elders that rule well be counted worthy of double honor, especially they who labor in the word and doctrine" (1 Tim. 5:17).

This advice of Paul's referred particularly to those elders in the local church who "labored" to teach effectively the great truths of God's Word to their people. Such men surely deserve special honor and appreciation.

It is not unreasonable to apply the same principle to those "elders" of our great nation who have labored diligently to obtain and preserve the biblical principles which have so blessed our sweet land of liberty ever since its beginning. There have been many such great leaders, but the two who probably made the most significant contributions were the two presidents whom we specially honor on Presidents' Day — George Washington and Abraham Lincoln.

Neither man was particularly "religious" in worship or lifestyle, yet both men believed in God and creation, and both were men who prayed for wisdom and guidance in the establishment and preservation of our nation.

It is interesting that both were given names with biblical connotations. "George" is from a Greek word meaning "tiller and dresser of the soil" and "Abraham" from a Hebrew word meaning "father of multitudes."

In considering these men and their names, we note that the first man Adam was placed by God "into the garden of Eden to dress it and to keep it," whereas the first man ever named Abraham was promised to be "a father of many nations" (Gen. 2:15; 17:5). Yet it was George Washington who is called "the father of his country," and Abraham Lincoln who was chosen to "keep the union."

In any case, both presidents (as well as many others) surely "ruled well" and are "worthy of double honor" on what has, sadly, become for most people just another holiday.

THE PRESIDENT'S HEART

"The king's heart is in the hand of the LORD, as the rivers of water: he turneth it whithersoever he will" (Prov. 21:1).

A river may seem to meander aimlessly, but it eventually reaches its goal. The twists and turns along the way are constrained by a variety of hydraulic and geologic factors that determine its local speed and direction, but somehow it "just keeps rolling along" toward the sea.

So it is with a king, or with a president, or any leader of a state or nation. He may have a goal in mind (honorable or otherwise) for the nation he governs, but there are numerous people and circumstances along the way that will either impede or help his progress toward that goal. In fact, we ourselves — the Christian citizens of his nation — are an integral component of those circumstances.

The president's heart is in the hands of God. In fact, "the powers that be are ordained of God" (Rom. 13:1). Whether the ruler comes into power by election or inheritance or coup d'etat or some other way (depending upon the nation and type of government), God is in control and will accomplish *His* ultimate goal.

That is why it is vital that we frequently make "supplications, prayers, intercessions, and giving of thanks . . . for all men," especially for "kings, and for all that are in authority" so that we will all be able to "lead a quiet and peaceable life in all godliness and honesty" (1 Tim. 2:1–2).

Our American nation has had many great men as our presidents over the years, and many of our ancestors were indeed men and women of prayer. We do have a great heritage in our nation of both leaders and followers who believed in the Creator God of the Bible and who prayed diligently for their country and the great decisions of its history. We must — *must* — do the same today!

For Such a
Time as This

"For if thou altogether holdest thy peace at this time, then shall there enlargement and deliverance arise to the Jews from another place; but thou and thy father's house shall be destroyed: and who knoweth whether thou art come to the kingdom for such a time as this?" (Esther 4:14).

This great challenge to Queen Esther by her uncle, Mordecai, urging her to be willing to risk her own life to save the lives of her people, embodies a timeless principle which has challenged many another man or woman of God in later times. One thinks of Paul, for example, who could testify that "what things were gain to me, those I counted loss for Christ" (Phil. 3:7), and whom, therefore, God used greatly in the critical times of the early church.

Then there were Wycliffe and Hus and Martin Luther and many others in post-biblical times who, like Paul, could say: "Neither count I my life dear unto myself, so that I might finish my course with joy, and the ministry, which I have received of the Lord Jesus" (Acts 20:24).

Furthermore, this special calling of men for special ministries at critical times is not limited to preachers and evangelists (consider Queen Esther!). Surely George Washington, "the father of his country" was such a man, and so were Abraham Lincoln and many others.

Who, therefore, is to say that the same principle does not apply, at least in some measure, to everyone? Our role in history may not be as strategic and far-reaching as that of Queen Esther or George Washington, but God does have a high calling in mind, and a vital ministry of some sort, for everyone. The great tragedy is that most people "hold their peace" when it comes to taking a vital and dangerous stand for God and His truth, and therefore "enlargement and deliverance" have to be raised up by Him "from another place."

May God help each of us, called as we are to some significant ministry which only we can perform "at such a time as this" to be able to say with Esther, "If I perish, I perish" (Esther 4:16), but also with Paul, "I have fought a good fight, I have finished my course, I have kept the faith" (2 Tim. 4:7).

Watch and Be Sober

"Therefore let us not sleep, as do others; but let us watch and be sober" (1 Thess. 5:6).

On each anniversary of Pearl Harbor Day, with also the more recent (September 11, 2001) attack on the twin towers of the World Trade Center in our memories, we still need often to be reminded that watchfulness and sobriety are of high importance in a dangerous world. Despite many indications that our forces were vulnerable to sudden destruction on that terrible morning over 60 years ago, the attack on Pearl Harbor came suddenly on many who were sleeping and unprepared. More recently, the many warning signs of imminent terrorist attacks by Koran-believing Muslims on key American targets had likewise been largely ignored, and business-as-usual was being carried on in New York and Washington, apparently oblivious to the imminent massacres soon coming from the sky.

This indifferent attitude still seems prevalent among much of the nation, although our president and other leaders have tried to awaken the sleepers. Our nation needs to watch and pray, as never before, but an anti-spiritual humanistic fog seems to have enveloped our land.

Our text above is primarily directed to individual Christian believers, of course. *We* need to watch and be sober, not only on behalf of our nation, but also for our communities, our families, and ourselves. "Be sober, be vigilant; because your adversary the devil, as a roaring lion, walketh about, seeking whom he may devour" (1 Pet. 5:8).

Satan has great power in this world, but "greater is he that is in you, than he that is in the world" (1 John 4:4). The apostle Peter would join with the apostle Paul (author of our text above) in his exhortation, reminding us that "the end of all things is at hand: be ye therefore sober, and watch unto prayer" (1 Pet. 4:7).

WHEN THE
HORSEMEN RIDE

"If thou hast run with the footmen, and they have wearied thee, then how canst thou contend with horses? and if in the land of peace, wherein thou trustedst, they wearied thee, then how wilt thou do in the swelling of Jordan?" (Jer. 12:5).

It is relatively easy in a land of religious freedom such as ours to live and witness for the Lord, but the time may well come when that freedom will be lost, and one can only serve the Lord openly at great risk. There are many countries in the world today where it is physically dangerous to take a strong Christian stand, and it is not unlikely that such a condition will prevail here too one of these days.

If such a time should come to America, how would Christians behave? Would they be careless and sleeping, as so many were on Pearl Harbor Day over 60 years ago? The frightening aspect of today's Christian community is that, with so few willing to stand for God's truth against mere intellectual attacks, what will they do when real persecution comes? When Christians compromise so readily with modern evolutionary humanism, will they one day actually surrender to the enemy when godless atheism reigns? How many would choose to receive "the mark . . . of the beast" rather than the martyr's "crown of life" (Rev. 13:17; 2:10), if such a choice should be faced?

America's leaders today, time after time, have been caught off guard by terrorist actions, just as they were at Pearl Harbor. Time after time, nothing is done for fear of offending public opinion and America's enemies. Similarly, America's Christian leaders are intimidated into one unscriptural compromise after another whenever liberals and humanists launch public attacks on biblical positions.

When the horsemen ride and the floods overflow, how will we do?

A Day
of Infamy

"That day is a day of wrath, a day of trouble and distress, a day of wasteness and desolation, a day of darkness and gloominess, a day of clouds and thick darkness" (Zeph. 1:15).

Senior citizens over 65 years of age well remember Pearl Harbor Day, December 7, 1941, when the Japanese largely destroyed America's Pacific Fleet in a surprise attack on our ships safely anchored and resting in the bay at Honolulu. The president of the nation, Franklin D. Roosevelt, went on national radio, calling that Sunday morning "a day of infamy." Soon our nation was a full combatant in the remaining four years of the terrible World War II.

The Bible tells us of a coming "day" whose destructions and slaughters will far exceed any event of the past — except for the world-destroying deluge in the time of Noah. That coming day is called the "Day of the Lord." It will begin on a literal day, of course, but will continue for several more years before the judgments of God will cease and world peace can finally be established. God has allowed men much freedom for many thousands of years, but eventually God will step in and say, in effect, "That's enough." It will finally be *His* day!

There is much in His written Word warning us of the terrible judgments scheduled for our unbelieving world in *that day*. We do not know how soon that day of wrath and trouble, distress, and desolation will begin, but the signs of its imminence are multiplying, and men and women who are wise ought to be preparing.

As Paul wrote to Christians long ago, "Ye, brethren, are not in darkness, that that day should overtake you as a thief" (1 Thess. 5:4). As John wrote, "Abide in him; that, when he shall appear, we may . . . not be ashamed before him at his coming" (1 John 2:28).

KING
OF PEACE

"And Melchizedek king of Salem brought forth bread and wine: and he was the priest of the most high God" (Gen. 14:18).

The mysterious king Melchizedek was at least a type — if not an actual pre-incarnate appearance — of Christ. As such, it is appropriate that he is called the "King of Salem," or "King of peace," and that this is the first mention of the word "peace" (Hebrew, *Shalem,* or *Shalom*) in the Bible. He is also called "King of righteousness" (Heb. 7:2), because his name is a combination of two Hebrew words carrying this meaning.

Thus, Melchizedek — that is, in principle, Jesus Christ — is king of both peace and righteousness, for neither can really exist without the other. True peace can be founded only in true righteousness, for "there is no peace, saith the Lord, unto the wicked" (Isa. 48:22). Similarly, God had promised, "O that thou hadst hearkened to my commandments! then had thy peace been as a river, and thy righteousness as the waves of the sea" (Isa. 48:18).

Peace and righteousness go together. No armistice or peace treaty will ever be permanent (always there is a new "Pearl Harbor Day" ahead) unless founded on righteousness, and this will never be until Christ returns, for He is both the "Prince of Peace" and "the righteousness of God" (Isa. 9:6; 2 Cor. 5:21). The nations of the world have been at war with God, and therefore with each other, ever since sin entered the world. When He does return, there will finally be permanent peace and eternal righteousness. "In his days Judah shall be saved, and Israel shall dwell safely: and this is his name whereby he shall be called, THE LORD OUR RIGHTEOUSNESS" (Jer. 23:6).

We may well honor those who have fought and died for peace, as did those who died for our country, but real and permanent peace can only be attained through the King of Peace.

WHENCE
COME WARS

"From whence come wars and fighting among you? come they not hence, even of your lusts that war in your members?" (James 4:1).

One of the perennial questions raised by skeptics is, "Why does God allow war in His world, if He is really a God of love and power?" Most of our personal lives have been profoundly affected by war, directly or indirectly. Those in the older generation all remember keenly, for example, just where they were on December 7, 1941 (Pearl Harbor Day), and how it changed their lives. Even now, over 60 years later, the events of September 11, 2001, are repeatedly being compared to *that* date, as another "day of infamy," as President Roosevelt called it 60-plus years ago.

God gives a deeper insight on the cause of wars than just blaming Hitler or Osama or some other powerful human leader. He says we are all to blame. The "lusts that war" in our own minds and bodies lead to personal conflicts, and these to group conflicts, and ultimately to deadly combat between nations. Thus, wars are going to continue in the world as long as there is sin in the world.

Every person, therefore, whether American or Russian, Jew or Arab, is by nature a warmonger, not a peacemaker. Yet Jesus "made peace through the blood of his cross . . . to reconcile all things unto himself" (Col. 1:20). Before there can be true peace between man and man, there must be real peace between man and God.

Thus, the only real way we can be peacemakers individually is to do what we can to bring men to Christ. He has given us "the ministry of reconciliation" as "ambassadors for Christ," and we must beseech all men "in Christ's stead, be ye reconciled to God" (2 Cor. 5:18, 20). Until Christ himself returns as Prince of Peace, there is no other effective way.

REMEMBER

"Yea, I think it meet, as long as I am in this tabernacle, to stir you up by putting you in remembrance" (2 Pet. 1:13).

"Remember the Alamo!" was the battle cry which stirred up the Texas patriots in their battle for independence from Mexico. During the Spanish-American War, the cry was "Remember the Maine!" The surprise Japanese attack on the Pacific fleet inspired the World War II slogan "Remember Pearl Harbor!"

To many, Pearl Harbor Day still "stirs up" remembrances as we recall the many fathers, friends, and loved ones who sacrificed their lives in defense of liberty during those memorable years. It is good to remember the martyrs and heroes who have gone before, for those who do not learn from history will eventually find themselves repeating history.

The apostle Peter (in his last epistle) was especially concerned that his readers remember all the great evidences of the Christian faith and the great principles of the Christian life: "Wherefore I will not be negligent to put you always in remembrance of these things, though ye know them, and be established in the present truth" (2 Pet. 1:12).

Then, anticipating his coming martyrdom, he stressed, "Moreover I will endeavor that ye may be able after my decease to have these things always in remembrance" (2 Pet. 1:15). Finally, "This second epistle, beloved, I now write unto you; in both which I stir up your pure minds by way of remembrance: That ye may be mindful of the words which were spoken before by the holy prophets, and of the commandment of us the apostles of the Lord and Saviour" (2 Pet. 3:1–2).

It is good to be "stirred up" to patriotic sacrifice by remembrance of those who have provided and preserved our American liberties, but it is still more important to have our minds (not just our emotions!) stirred up by remembrance of the wonderful works of God.

OUR
PERSONAL WAR

"For though we walk in the flesh, we do not war after the flesh" (2 Cor. 10:3).

A day over 60 years ago marked the entrance of our nation into the terrible World War II, the fading memories of which were recently stirred up by the dubious "Pearl Harbor" movie and then by the unspeakable attack on America on September 11, 2001. What this strange war on terrorism will bring in days to come we do not know, but we must trust in God and try to discern and follow His will, both nationally and individually.

For each of us is also in a perpetual spiritual war. In fact, the whole world system is at war with its Maker, and its commander-in-chief is Satan, the "god of this world" (2 Cor. 4:4). Paul exhorts us to "Put on the whole armor of God, that ye may be able to stand against the wiles of the devil" (Eph. 6:11) because, as Peter says, "your adversary the devil, as a roaring lion, walketh about, seeking whom he may devour" (1 Pet. 5:8).

This war we are in with Satan is not a war to be fought with bullets, or even with ballots. "(For the weapons of our warfare are not carnal, but mighty through God to the pulling down of strong holds;) Casting down imaginations, and every high thing that exalteth itself against the knowledge of God, and bringing into captivity every thought to the obedience of Christ" (2 Cor. 10:4–5).

At least a portion of this war must be fought and won daily within our own souls — and then we can do battle with Satan more effectively for the souls of those still deceived by him. Clad in God's spiritual armor (see Eph. 6:14–16), and wielding "the sword of the Spirit, which is the word of God: Praying always with all prayer and supplication in the Spirit" (Eph. 6:17–18), we indeed can each be "a good soldier of Jesus Christ" (2 Tim. 2:3).

INDEX OF ARTICLES

TEXT VERSES

ALL SCRIPTURES MENTIONED